INFANTRY OF THE LINE

T. J. GANDER

LONDON

IAN ALLAN LTD

Frontispiece:
TA soldiers on exercise helping each other over a wire fence. *MoD*

First published 1988

ISBN 0 7110 1788 3

Published by Ian Allan Ltd, Shepperton, Surrey; and printed by Ian Allan Printing Ltd at their works at Coombelands in Runnymede, England

All uncredited photographs are the copyright of the Author.

Contents

Introduction

This book is an account of how the modern British Infantry is organised, how it works, how it is trained and how it is equipped. It deals primarily with the British Army's Line Regiments that have given the nation such excellent service over the centuries and which continue to form a major portion of the Army to this day. The book will not deal with the Brigade of Guards or the Parachute Regiment — they are dealt with in ample detail elsewhere, but much of the equipment and other detail covered here can be related to them as well as to their Line colleagues.

It might seem strange to the casual reader of military topics that a book on the British Infantry is felt necessary at all. A quick look around any military library will soon reveal tome after tome relating to Infantry regiments and Infantry topics. A closer examination will soon reveal that almost all of them deal with either historical topics or lump the Infantry with some other topic, again usually with a historical bent. This book is different for it relates to how the Infantry are *now*. It goes into details of their current organisation, working methods, equipment and training. Their history is but touched upon for it is well covered elsewhere.

A study of the modern Infantry is very apposite at the moment for as at many other points in their long development and history, the Infantry are in a state of transition. New equipment, organisational procedures and operating methods are being introduced to a confusing extent as far as the military observer is concerned, and those involved are sometimes no less bewildered. However, the changes are taking place in an atmosphere of acceptance and even eagerness that would seem unthinkable to the restricted military outlook of only a few decades ago. During one not-so-distant period, whenever the word 'change' was introduced to a certain strata of military society the result was akin to an explosion of reaction.

Reactions these days are much milder and more tolerant of change. They have to be, for the Infantry is now operating as part of an Army that is small in numbers, even if its importance seems to grow rather than diminish. Although the numbers remain relatively stable these days the commitments do not, so the Infantry can still be encountered scattered at odd points around the globe, policing, standing guard, supporting the local authorities and all the while training, training and then training some more.

As will be related later in this book the British Infantry retain their importance to the Army as a whole to the point where the British Army is an Infantry Army. Thus to understand the Army of today we have to start with the Infantry. From them everything else within the British military land establishment emanates, including their operating standards, pride in themselves and their job, commitment to the tasks in hand, and everything else. The reasons why this remains so can be found in these pages.

Acknowledgements

In the compilation of this book the Author has received considerable assistance and gained much knowledge — nearly all of which was provided by the Infantry themselves. The Director of Infantry and the Staff of the School of Infantry have been the source of a great deal of assistance and guidance in many forms and the mere gratitude of the Author is insufficient thanks for all their help at all levels. I can only hope that they will find this book worthy of all their efforts.

Glossary of Abbreviations

AAC	Army Air Corps
AATC	All Arms Tactics Course
ACC	Army Catering Corps
AIMI	Armoured Infantry Manning Increment
AITAT	Armoured Infantry Training Advisory Team
APC	Armoured personnel carrier
APDS	Armour piercing discarding sabot
APSE	Armour piercing secondary effects
APTC	Army Physical Training Corps
ARRV	Armoured repair and recovery vehicle
Asslt	Assault
ATAF	Allied Tactical Air Force
AVRE	Armoured Vehicle Royal Engineers
BAOR	British Army of the Rhine
BATCO	Battle Group Commander
BAV	Battery command vehicle
BE	Belgian
BICS	Battlefield Information and Command System

Below:
A FV432 on the Suffield ranges in Canada.

Bn	Battalion
BSC	British Support Corps
BR	British
CASS	Camouflage Support System
Cat	Catering
CEPA	Charging Equipment Pure Air
COTC	Commanding Officers Tactics Course
Coy	Company
CVR(T)	Combat vehicle reconnaissance (tracked)
CWS	Common Weapon Sight
DEFWES	Direct Firer Weapons Effect Simulators
Det	Detachment
DPM	Disruptive pattern material
FFLAV	Future Families of Light Armoured Vehicles
FIBUA	Fighting in built-up areas
FOO	Forward Observation Officer
FP	Fire Post
FSC	Ferret Scout Car
FV	Field Vehicle
GE	German
GPALEP	General Purpose Anti-laser Eye Protection
GPMG	General purpose machine gun
HE	High explosive
HEAT	High explosive anti-tank
HQ	Headquarters
HMG	Heavy machine gun
HMLC	High Mobility Load Carrier
Hz	Hertz
IGB	Inner German Border
IRG	Immediate Replenishment Group
ISO	International Standards Organisation
ITDU	Infantry Trials and Development Unit
IW	Individual Weapon
IWS	Infantry Weapons Sight
LAD	Light Aid Detachment
LAW	Light Anti-armour Weapon
LMG	Light machine gun
LSW	Light Support Weapon
MAOV	Mechanised artillery observation vehicle
MCV	Mechanised combat vehicle
MCT	Milan Compact Turret
MFC	Mortar Fire Control
Mob	Mobile
Mor	Mortar
NATO	North Atlantic Treaty Organisation
NBC	Nuclear, biological and chemical
NCO	Non-commissioned officer
NITAT	Northern Ireland Training Advisory Team
NORTHAG	Northern Army Group
OR	Other Ranks
OTIS	Observer Thermal Imaging System
PC	Permanent Cadre
PCBC	Platoon Commanders Battle Course
Pl	Platoon
PLC	Personal Load Carrier
Pnr	Pioneer
PSAO	Permanent Staff Administration Officer
PSBC	Platoon Sergeants Battle Course
PSI	Permanent Staff Instructor
QM	Quartermaster
RA	Royal Artillery
RAC	Royal Armoured Corps
RAFG	Royal Air Force Germany
RAMC	Royal Army Medical Corps
RAPC	Royal Army Pay Corps
RAW	Rifleman's Assault Weapon
RE	Royal Engineers
Recce	Reconnaissance
REME	Royal Electrical and Mechanical Engineers
RMAS	Royal Military Academy Sandhurst
RSA	Royal School of Artillery
RUC	Royal Ulster Constabulary
SACLOS	Semi-automatic command line-of-sight
SASC	Small Arms School Corps
SAWES	Small Arms Weapons Effect Simulators
SCBS	Section Commanders Battle Course
SCHINF	School of Infantry
Sect	Section
SF	Sustained fire
Sigs	Signals
SLR	Self-loading Rifle
SOTC	Senior Officers Training Course
Sp	Support
SUIT	Sight Unit Infantry Trilux
SUSAT	Sight Unit Small Arms Trilux
SRI	Short Range Insert
TA	Territorial Army
TAG	Training Advisory Group
TAOR	Territorial Area of Responsibility
TCW	Thermal Camouflage Woodland
UDR	Ulster Defence Regiment
UKLF	United Kingdom Land Forces
UKMF(L)	United Kingdom Mobile Force (Land)
VCP	Vehicle check point
W	Watts
WO	Warrant Officer
WP	White phosphorus

1 The Modern Infantry

Any account relating to the modern Infantry has to present two disparate facts. The first is that the basic role of the modern Infantry is exactly what it has been for hundreds of years, namely to close with the enemy and destroy their will and ability to fight. A basic enough premise on which to build perhaps but this has to be balanced by the fact that the way the modern Infantry goes about its tasks bears no comparison whatsoever to the operational methods in use a relatively short time ago.

Yet there are points of strong contact between the modern Infantry and their forebears. Some of these points of contact are so marked that they continue to make an impact on the character not only of the Infantry but of the British Army itself. The British Army continues to be, in the main, an infantry army. The Regular and Territorial Infantry still form nearly one third of the manpower within the modern Army and this alone continues to mark the British Army with its unique character to the extent that its standards and repute are set overall by the Infantry. These standards are such that today, the very spirit and will to fight of the British Army is reflected directly from the Infantry battalions and is diffused throughout every command and operating level.

This stamp of the Infantry character has always been present wherever and whenever the British Army has operated. Other armies such as that of the Soviet Union might identify their artillery as their proudest Arm and the Bundeswehr their armoured troops, but the British Army continues in its unique fashion to rest its reputation in the eyes of the world in its Infantry. The very nature of the British Infantry is still the British Army's greatest strength and lasting quality at a time when it would seem that mechanised warfare has reduced the individual soldier to the existence of a mere cog in a military machine. This attitude completely overlooks the fact that in any form of warfare the soldier's weapons and equipment, mechanised or otherwise, are only as good as the soldier who uses them. In the British Infantry that soldier has always been as good as he can be, and that good has frequently meant excellent. From that excellence has stemmed the sterling qualities of the British Army itself — qualities that have served the nation well in the past and which continue to serve well today.

These high standards within the modern Infantry are due to several factors. One is that today the Infantry have at their disposal a wider range of weapons and equipment than at any time throughout their history. Not only does the Infantry soldier have at his disposal a greater array of modern weapons, but he also has more of them. Once upon a time the Infantry used their rifles and little else. Today they still have their rifles, but in addition there are also machine guns, mortars, anti-tank guided missiles and mobile fire platforms such as the Warrior infantry combat vehicle. There are also radios, NBC equipments, reconnaissance vehicles, trucks, assault engineer equipment, and so on. To go with this hardware there is a corresponding array of skills and abilities to use the potential of each item to the full. This is something else that the Infantry shares with the rest of the Army.

Right:
LAW 80 in action. *Hunting Engineering*

Above:
Warrior, the Infantry's new combat vehicle at speed.

The Infantry soldier of today is far more advanced in ability compared to his counterpart of the past. Today he is a skilled technician with education and capability levels far above those of years gone by.

Yet all these skills, weapon qualities and standards, together with that higher level of individual intellectual ability, are of no use to any soldier who lacks one basic requirement — the will and ability to fight. In short the Infantry are there to destroy their enemy. That takes something more than just good weapons, equipment and training. There has to be that something extra that enables a man to stand up on a battlefield and move against an adversary who, in his turn, is doing his level best to remove *his* will and ability to fight. Such deliberate actions demand a level of moral determination and toughness that has always been a special characteristic of the British Infantry, and remains so today. These military virtues also demand a high

level of leadership to employ them to their full potential.

The British foot soldier has a military record of dour toughness and dogged ability that few nations can match. Exactly why this should be can be initially answered by examining the motivations that produce the will to fight. These are many and complex but they can generally be summarised by two examples. The first is common to everyone, although it is often sublimated to a considerable degree. It is the wish to preserve personal freedoms of action, especially within a family bonding. In short this can be regarded as fighting for a cause, and the more personal and direct the threat to that cause, the greater the will to fight. For the British Infantry soldier this can mean the immediate family of wife, children and relations, but in the wider sense the 'family' can include the battalion itself. This brings into play the second important reason that provides the motivation to fight. This has been recognised as the preservation of the integrity and reputation of the individual soldier and of those around them. Again this raises the concept of the battalion being more than just a military organisation of individuals.

When a soldier joins an Infantry battalion he is joining a military organisation within which individuals learn to associate with one another to the point where reliance and regard between soldiers becomes more than just a bonding; it becomes the personal acceptance of a relationship that is to all intents and purposes a family grouping. Within this grouping the soldier comes to regard any enemy incursion or intrusion as a direct threat to his family establishment and reacts accordingly. The feeling of close association also engenders that spirit of preservation of personal and group integrity that is formed within a battalion. Some of this sense of integrity can be instilled into a battalion by the passing on of its history and traditions, but, during the final test in the heat of battle, these historical factors (although important) are overcome by the more direct will to protect one's own kind and preserve the individual soldier's qualities of self-esteem and the group's integrity, both between comrades and in the eye of outsiders.

The British Infantry has learned over the years that this self-motivating association of individuals can work very well. It has brought about that indefinable entity known as the Regimental System. In this system the close and continued association of individuals within what is virtually a closed society produces something that can be termed almost as a brotherhood. It has been repeatedly proved that such a brotherhood can work together successfully under whatever circumstances, good or bad, that a military career can bring. The system produces the required military virtues but they are nurtured within the battalion. The Regiment is an important figurehead organisation but in motivation terms it merely supplies the trappings such as the uniform, cap badge and tradition. The battalion provides the foundation for the real personal and continued bonding. There are several reasons why this should be but two are again more important than the rest.

The first is that the British Infantry, along with the rest of the Army, are full time professional soldiers, The transient influences of conscripts are thus not present as they are in so many other armies. Once a soldier joins his Infantry battalion he knows that he will remain there for years, and in many cases the battalion will be his military home for his entire Army career. He might leave it from time to time for training courses, or for special postings to other units, but the battalion is always there to act as a secure base to which he can return. Within the battalion he will make his personal friends, learn to respect and work with his commanders and other associates and from them he will acquire and assume the military qualities that makes the Infantry battalion such a unique society. Much of this assumption of conduct from others will be almost subliminal. Some will be learned almost by rote, but the best kind is that which is assumed by self-motivation. The end result is an individual who regards himself as part of an élite group that is very special, to the point where he feels and knows that he and his group have acquired high standards that will take some beating and in which he has invested his own pride and reputation. That most elusive of military qualities, leadership, also gains a richness and a special chance to prosper within this environment.

The British Regimental System can engender these finer qualities of military conduct by one further factor, and that is that they are inherently British. Just as the true nature of any national character is reflected in its legal system, so can it be found reflected in the nature of its armed forces. This truism has been stated and proved often enough over the years and it remains true of the British Army. Despite the various oddities of behaviour that have beset the United Kingdom over recent decades, the basic good nature and qualities of British society have remained remarkably unchanged. British individuals are at heart still good natured, fair minded, relatively unselfish and stolid. They are also conservative, docile, somewhat unimaginative and over-complacent to the point of exaggerated self-esteem. This brief (and incomplete) summary is also a list of some of the more desirable military virtues so they can be seen reflected within the British Army in general and the Infantry battalions in particular.

When these virtues are distilled within the Regimental System, the result is a fighting ability that few can match. Many overseas armed forces are currently trying to create the Regimental System within their own organisations by various means but are finding it hard going or even counter-productive. There is something that the British nation has that others lack. It can perhaps be summed up as an innate desire to form close and lasting associations from which others can be excluded. Whatever it is, it continues to produce within the Infantry battalions that corporate spirit that serves the nation so well.

In the summary of national characteristics provided above the word 'conservative' was used deliberately, for it continues to be one of the less attractive military virtues to this day. Any individual or association naturally likes to keep things as they are for as long as possible, not only for the sake of an easy life, but also for the reason that change can produce disruption, turbulence and uncertainty. An excess of conservatism was for long one of the sins demonstrated by the British Army of the past but it is one that can be attributed to the Infantry no longer.

The Infantry of today is a very flexible and free-thinking military organisation. It has to be, for the simple reason that, although now reduced in numbers, the Army still has to meet a number of continuing national commitments. This has led to a situation where there is now only a very limited reserve force on hand to meet any unexpected contingency that might arise. Thus any Infantry battalion could suddenly find itself taken out of its intended role and environment and placed in a situation where an entirely new set of operational and other criteria might apply. This has happened repeatedly over the last 40 years and, to illustrate the point, the events of 1982 in the South Atlantic are not all that distant in historical terms. Something of that nature might well crop up again. Thus, soldiers who might be busy training for one role can, and do, suddenly find themselves embroiled in operations far removed from those intended. This probability has led to one definition of the role of the modern Infantry being: 'To do whatever is required in whatever circumstances they find themselves.'

In such a situation, the last thing the Infantry can afford is conservatism in any form. They have therefore adopted in its place an accepted flexibility of approach to their job, plus the associated mental agility that actuates quick reactions, that few outside organisations can match. The list of major Infantry roles is wide and varied to a point that many outsiders would find daunting.

Top of the list is the role of armoured warfare on NATO's Central Front. In this role the Infantry operates as armoured and mechanised infantry in close co-operation with tanks, artillery and combat engineers to fight a major All Arms battle. In such a role the Infantry is a powerful partner of the other arms. Such operations demand and get a fair proportion of the Infantry's resources in men and equipment, and training for the role is involved and on-going. The introduction of Warrior will provide the Infantry with an improved capability to expand their role in this area.

Also part of the Army's commitment to NATO is their Infantry contribution to the reinforcement of the NATO flanks in an emergency and to the Allied Mobile Force (Land) in particular. It is this that might well involve the Infantry in the most sudden and involved alterations of environment and role. In these flank operations the Infantry is the lead arm.

The Infantry also carry out the greater, if not the entire, part of counter-terrorist and counter-insurgency operations. Needless to say this is typified by the Northern Ireland scenario but it should not be forgotten that over the years similar operations have been carried out in more distant regions. During these operations complete reversals of normal operating methods can arise. Restraint and patience are often the watchwords in place of dash and immediate reaction while leadership has to be conducted at the most junior of levels to a degree not normally encountered during other forms of operation.

The fourth of the Infantry's main roles is that of the garrison force. Despite the retreat from Empire during the years since 1945, there are still colonial outposts scattered around the globe that continue to require soldiers to be available to maintain local order and deter intrusions from outsiders. This is again an Infantry responsibility and consequently soldiers can still hope for postings to Hong Kong (a commitment that will be rescinded in 1997), Belize, Gibraltar or Cyprus. There is also the Berlin garrison to be maintained as part of the local 1945 Treaty arrangements. Although many of the duties involved in such locations are ceremonial, they allow time for detailed training in the basic skills. At the same time, as history has often shown, in such places things can alter dramatically almost overnight.

Quite apart from their military duties, the modern Infantry are now more closely associated with their local civilian communities than they have ever been. Many married soldiers now live with their families away from their barracks among the civilian population and build up local social relationships at all levels. These relationships are often further cemented when calamities such as natural disasters strike and the Infantry turn out to assist and provide relief operations, as happens from time to time. At more personal levels, Infantry units undertake charitable efforts in connection with local worthy causes, and even more personal are the relationships that lead to local marriages and other friendships. All these (not forgetting the sporting contacts that are often formed) are now on a scale that would have been unimaginable to the soldiers of previous generations when they were usually far down the generally-accepted social order. Those times are now long gone.

While social relationships with the civilian community are important for the modern soldier they are secondary to his main purpose in life which is the preparation for and conduct of combat. For the Infantry this involves constant hard training and variety in activities and surroundings. Anyone joining the modern Infantry can expect a wide variety of experiences and they can be

virtually certain of using their acquired skills in action at some stage or another of their Service careers. Whatever might arise one thing is certain. It is that whatever action might take place the Infantry will be in the thick of the fight.

There will also be the chance to travel, undertake sporting activities of all kinds and there is always the constant opportunity to assume new skills and levels of education, both military and academic. But all this is still secondary to the ability to fight when called upon to do so. That is when the true character and ubiquitous nature of the British Infantry soldier becomes really apparent. Then they will stand and fight, attack or simply wait and take on whatever happens with all the strength of character that has marked the British Infantry over the centuries. They will have at their disposal weapons and equipment that can tackle anything an enemy might throw at them, they have been trained to use their weapons to the full and under any circumstances, and all the time they have that cohesive fighting quality that only a long and continued association with their fellows can bring to combat.

Below:
The Saxon wheeled armoured personnel carrier.

2 The Infantry Since 1945

As the war clouds cleared from the Far East in August 1945 the war in Europe had already been over for some months. The British Army at last had time to look back over its wartime achievements and by and large could be well satisfied. After the usual shaky start the British soldier had suffered and endured much, but by much reliance on the usual traits of good humour, dogged tenacity and an ability to train and operate under a surprising variety of conditions, the fight was finally won.

Under the bright light of victory the reality that it had all been a very close thing was momentarily hidden. There was also an understandable tendency to overlook the fact that the war had been won only with the active co-operation of more powerful allies and that the conflict had left the nation drained of money, resources and the where-withal to continue to fight for very much longer without considerable assistance.

Unfortunately the world of 1945 was very different from that of 1918 when the Great War finally came to an end. The atomic bomb had made its debut and the seemingly overwhelming power of the air arm had made its mark to a devastating extent. There would be no going back to the halcyon days of 1939 or to the days where the Army could be a small and relatively inexpensive club of well-trained individuals that provided an armed force to defend the United Kingdom itself and prevent the British Empire from changing hands. The combination of the nuclear bomb and long range aircraft changed all that and it was only too obvious that the United Kingdom would be unable to fight any future major conflict alone.

Thus although the end of the war meant a reduction in the numbers of men in uniform it did not mean a return to the minimal prewar strengths that were so difficult to correct in 1940 and the years thereafter. The British Army, including the Infantry, remained strong in manpower, many of whom remained in Germany — not only as an occupation force but as a possible counter to the expansionist threat provided by the Soviet Union. They are still there for it was soon obvious that the postwar years would be far from peaceful.

Within the Army the Infantry had lost its numerical ascendancy. In 1939 the Infantry formed about half the Army's population in manpower terms, but such had been the technical and logistical demands of the warfare conducted between 1939 and 1945 that this proportion had shrunk to almost a quarter. The very nature of warfare had changed. By 1945, land conflict was a mobile undertaking with internal communications enabling the execution of operations on a scale that had hitherto been thought impossible. Warfare had been extended to the airborne sphere and in 1945 the British were once again masters of amphibious warfare.

For the foot soldier much had changed during the war years, but the soldier of 1918 would still have been able to find much that was familiar in 1945. The uniforms might have changed to the unglamorous and baggy battledress that was worn for virtually all occasions during the immediate postwar years, but the 1918 soldier would have recognised the No 4 0.303in rifle and indeed the old No 1 Mk 111 was still in use by many units. The Vickers machine gun was still in service and so was the familiar No 36 grenade. Set against that, the Bren Gun, which had gained itself an enviable reputation for reliability and efficiency as a light

machine gun, was unfamiliar and so was the functional-looking Sten sub-machine gun. Anti-tank guns were new and so was the array of wireless equipment that would have made many of the battles of attrition of World War 1 unnecessary had they been available at the time. Also new was the fact that the soldier of 1945 was already becoming familiar with no longer having to march everywhere. Mechanisation in the form of the truck and armoured vehicles such as the Universal Carrier had made the Infantry mobile on a scale unknown in 1918.

Although he did not know it at the time, the Infantryman of 1945 faced a far more uncertain future than his counterpart of

1918. Within months of the end of hostilities the British Infantry were once more in action, containing civil disturbances or various levels of guerilla warfare, in Trieste, Palestine and Greece and the responsibilities of Empire meant that it was not long before operations were in progress in Malaya. By 1950 the Korean War had begun and from then onwards the Army, and the Infantry in particular, was always on active service somewhere or other, be it in Kenya, Aden, Cyprus or Egypt, among many other locations.

The year 1945 heralded the end of two familiar peacetime factors of British Army life. They were the last effects of the Cardwell Reforms of the 1870s and the establishment of an all-professional Army. Dealing with the first factor, the Cardwell Reforms had established a regional recruiting system that provided most Infantry regiments with two battalions — one for training at home while the other policed part of the Empire. World War 2 strained that system to breaking point for it meant that each Infantry regiment was in effect its own little organisation that had to be slotted somehow into a larger organisation. Many staff planners envied the way that other armies, and the Germans in particular, were able to rapidly organise *ad hoc* units from whatever manpower and materiel was to hand in a way that the British Regimental System seemed unable to match. Some pundits even stated the heresy that the establishment of a Corps of Infantry would go some way to correct what was by 1945 a historical organisational anomaly. Even in 1945 the British Army was still, in many ways, the 'collection of regiments' that it had long been considered by many overseas counterparts. Set against that was the fierce pride generated by the British system that so often produced remarkable results in action, so after 1945, when a decrease in manpower

was ordained, it was made by simply scrapping the two-battalion establishment and making each regiment a single battalion entity. Some regiments were made to amalgamate, usually with only a minimum of fuss and disruption, but by and large the Regimental System remained intact for a while longer.

The second novel factor after 1945 was the use of conscription in peacetime. By 1947 it was realised that the level of postwar commitments for the Army could not be met by volunteers for the Regular Army alone, so by 1947 what came to be known as National Service was introduced and was largely accepted by the civilian population. Initially the term of service was one year, which was later extended to 18 months. By 1950, when the Korean War began, it was two years.

By 1949 the Infantry had 77 battalions, including the Guards and the Parachute Regiment, so many of the Army's conscripts found themselves in the Infantry. The bulk of them 'served their time' with stoical endurance, others used their two years to learn something new and contributed by their education and the injection of fresh ideas or approaches, while some even saw action in Malaya or elsewhere. Too many became casualties. Conscription was not ended until 1963, but by then it was no longer deemed necessary on anything like the previous scale.

After 1945 the British Empire gradually

contracted as newly-independent nations made their debut. The greatest change came in 1947 when the old British India became India and Pakistan. They were only two of the old British colonies that were handed over to their own governments during the postwar years. With India self-governing there was no longer any need for the string of colonies and coaling stations that had once been necessary to guard the Imperial route to the sub-continent, so the British Army withdrew from Egypt and many other long-established postings. During the series of withdrawals it was often the hapless Infantry who had to attempt to keep a semblance of order in being as, in too many places, various warring factions sought to gain power or ensure that the British left as soon as possible.

With those commitments gone there was no longer the need for vast reserves of manpower and the way was cleared for the return of an all-professional Army. That had been heralded in the Sandys White Paper of 1957 — a document that was to become regarded as infamous in many ways, but which nevertheless attempted to rationalise the United Kingdom's defence posture at a time when its resources were shrinking. The size of the Army was to be cut by half. The Infantry's 77 battalions were to be cut to 64. This led to a further round of regiments and battalions being merged and resulted in new regimental titles. To provide a semblance of rationalisation, groups of battalions were organised into 'brigades'.

The Infantry was also in the throes of re-equipment by 1957. It had entered the Korean War armed and equipped much as it had been in 1945 and after the initial encounters the war settled down into a conflict along virtually static fronts that would have been familiar to any Infantryman who took part in the long flog through Italy from 1943 to 1945. The Korean War highlighted the need for new weapons, and a new rifle in particular, but in fact that need had been recognised as early as 1945. In that year the development of a self-loading rifle had been combined with the instigation of a new rifle calibre which was to emerge as 0.280in. The new rifle emerged as the EM-2, but it was not accepted for political reasons when the Americans virtually enforced the acceptance of their 7.62mm × 51 cartridge on to the newly-formed North Atlantic Treaty Organisation (NATO), of which the United Kingdom was a member from its formation in 1949. The Infantry thus began to be issued with a British version of the Belgian FAL rifle, later to become the L1A1, from about 1955 onwards.

It was not the only new weapon. The 6-pounder and even larger 17-pounder anti-tank guns were replaced by lighter and handier 120mm recoilless guns, and by 1963 the old Vickers machine gun had finally been retired in favour of another weapon with a

Left:
A soldier of the Royal Scots trains in Northern Greece in 1973. *MoD*

Far left:
Men of the Royal Welch Fusiliers on jungle training in Belize during the early 1970s. *MoD*

Right:
**On the development path to
SA80, soldiers demonstrate
the first version of the
4.85mm Individual and
Light Support Weapons
during their first public
outing at the School of
Infantry.** *MoD*

Belgian origin — the General Purpose Machine Gun (GPMG), later to be known as the L7A2. By the early 1960s, the first of the long-lived FV432 armoured personnel carriers were being issued, but they were only part of a general updating and re-equipment programme for the Infantry instigated by experience gained in Korea.

By the early 1960s the bulk of the Infantry were located in West Germany as part of the overall NATO force. Then came one of the most traumatic reorganisations of the Infantry during any of the post-1945 years. In 1964 the Infantry was forced to accept the unwelcome fact that many regiments had to amalgamate and form themselves into 'divisions' for administration and recruiting purposes. The change was made by the government then in power primarily to save on defence spending and, accordingly, the names of many famous regiments passed into history and the Infantry had to get used to new regimental titles and multiple groupings of larger battalions. The division system has lasted to this day and the new battalions' names have been accepted, but in many messes attempts are still made to maintain the titles and traditions of long-gone regiments.

Around this time a belated change in combat tactics was introduced with the inauguration of the Combat Team and the Battle Group. The first uses of these for-

mations were made somewhat tentatively but they marked the first major stages in the evolution of the 'All-Arms Battle' concept within the British Army.

If that was not enough innovation, the old Territorial Army was reorganised and reduced in strength. In the process it became an integral part of the Regular Army as a reinforcement force for BAOR in addition to carrying out its time-honoured role of acting as a home defence force.

By the late 1960s, things were settling down and proceeding relatively smoothly — as far as life in the Infantry can ever be called smooth — and 1968 was the only year during this century when no British Army soldier was killed on active service. However, that situation altered drastically the year after when the current round of Northern Ireland troubles commenced. They have continued over since and over the years Northern Ireland has been a considerable drain on the Army's resources. As usual the Infantry had to bear the brunt of the constant policing, patrols, searches, riot control and generally partaking in that most unloved of military activities, namely 'Duties in Support of a Civil Power'. At times, the keeping of the peace in Ulster diverted men from NATO and other commitments to the point where cost-cutting attempts made during the mid-1970s to reduce the size of the Army by as many as 15,000 men had to be revised. Even so, the

Infantry, which by then had contracted to 55 battalions, was over-stretched and many battalions were well below their proper strengths.

The contraction was made with the usual welter of reorganisations and led to the 2nd Infantry Division being withdrawn from Germany, even though it remains part of BAOR (much of its manpower is now provided by the TA). A slight improvement in the numbers of men that could be recruited enabled battalion establishments to stabilise at something like their present levels. Gradually matters improved and projects to introduce new equipment and weapons were initiated. Guided weapons in the form of the non-operational Vigilant were used to provide invaluable handling experience ready for the time when advanced equipments such as Milan could be obtained. The lengthy project that was to lead to the Warrior infantry combat vehicle was initiated. The Infantry gained an integral reconnaissance element for every battalion and its support weapon structure was improved and strengthened. Training and the provision of the appropriate clothing and other equipment provided the capability to operate under NBC conditions to an extent that would have been thought impossible only a few years previously.

From time to time during the 1970s the Army, and the Infantry in particular, was called upon to carry out various forms of active operations in Cyprus and elsewhere and often provided assistance in the aftermath of natural disasters in some odd corners of the old Empire. Northern Ireland gradually ceased to be a major undertaking in Infantry terms as major subversion settled down to the current level of terrorist activity that can usually be contained by the local security forces. It seemed as though things were settling down yet again when Argentina invaded the Falkland Islands in 1982.

The successful conclusion of that campaign has had quite an effect on the Infantry in operational and equipment terms. It indicated that the level of individual fitness and training maintained over the years was correct and the operational encounters demonstrated the need for new weapons and operating methods. Some of these lessons were still being processed in 1988 and their end products may not be seen or appreciated for years to come.

In the meantime, new weapons and equipment continue to be issued to the Infantry. The issue of the new IW and LSW is now well under way and Warrior is in prospect. The latter could be the partial source of yet another reshuffle in Infantry organisation for the skills involved in operating Warrior may well mean the extension of Infantry battalion tours from the current three years to six. To the layman this sounds a simple enough measure, but for the Infantry it is a major change with many ramifications for not only Warrior battalions will be involved. It means that Home Defence battalions will retain their role for six years as well as will battalions trained for possible out-of-Europe operations. Already voices are being raised that the hallowed Regimental System is once more under threat, but in answer it could be stated that if a Corps of Infantry had been established when the opportunities were available in the past, the arguments would by now be hypothetical and the necessary changes now being considered could be made without difficulty.

Below:
Training on the Suffield Ranges in Canada in 1977. *B. Quarrie*

3 The Infantry Battalion

The Infantry Battalion is first and foremost a combat organisation. To the officers and other ranks who form the battalion it is more than just that, for the battalion provides them with a fixed environmental base that is the source of their social relationships, training, career opportunities and pride in themselves and their Service. It is to the battalion that a soldier is posted as a newly-commissioned officer or a newly-trained recruit, it is from within the battalion that the bulk of his military elementary education and training will be given and it is the battalion that comes to be regarded as a home — not in accommodation terms but rather as a fixed and stable base from where a Service career can be built. Many soldiers have spent their entire Service careers within the one battalion, while others use the battalion as a location which they can leave and perhaps return to as their career paths progress.

In organisational terms the battalion has to be regarded primarily as a combat formation, even though it may operate in battle as a cohesive unit only infrequently. The reasons for this seeming anomaly come from the nature of that combat formation innovation, the Battle Group. In any future major conflict the British Army is unlikely to be assembled on the battlefield in the neat and tidy establishments of battalions and regiments as in the past. These days each particular battlefield task is met by an All-Arms assemblage of units, with each particular component tailored in size and equipment levels to meet a particular combat requirement as closely as possible. Each of these All-Arms groupings is known as a Battle Group, which may be commanded by either the Infantry or Armour commander involved. A typical Battle Group would include formations from the Infantry, Armour, Artillery and Engineers, with further support provided by the Army Air Corps (AAC) and other Arms and Services as required. Individual Battle Groups would have their own particular mix of these formations. In one sector of a combat zone a Battle Group might be formed from an entire Infantry battalion with corresponding elements from the other Arms. In another sector the Infantry increment might be based upon a single company with much larger contributions from the Armour and Artillery. There is no hard-and-fast establishment for a Battle Group and Armoured or Infantry Battle Groups can exist. Each is formed to meet a particular situation and is structured accordingly.

For logistic purposes, the Battle Group is split into echelons. The men and vehicles who are involved in the actual fighting form the F Echelon and for administrative purposes the F Echelon includes the REME LAD vehicles and company ambulances.

The main supply component is known as the A Echelon which has its transport resources divided into two parts. The A1 Echelon looks after the supply needs of the F Echelon as they arise from hour to hour. In contrast the A2 Echelon supplies the A1 Echelon as its own supplies are issued. The A2 Echelon may be formed from the various company vehicles, plus vehicles from Royal Corps of Transport Immediate Replenishment Groups (IRG), and is usually located somewhere within the appropriate Forward Brigade Administrative Area. Less immediate logistic and other requirements are met by the B Echelon which handles matters such as pay, documentation, clothing and the

Above:
A Milan Firing Post in position ready to attack enemy armour. *MoD*

equipment of newly-arrived reservists and reinforcements. They operate from 4-tonne trucks located in the Divisional Administrative Area.

The Infantry battalion can be split up to meet the varied requirements of the Battle Group, but for the object of this description the Battalion will be described as an entity and in its peacetime form. In time of war various parts of any battalion might vary somewhat from the outlines provided below, but such variations are beyond the scope of this book.

There are four main types of Infantry battalion, plus a few variations. The most modern of these is the Armoured Infantry Battalion, the first of which had yet to be formed as these words were written. The Armoured Infantry Battalion is formed around the Warrior infantry combat vehicle, while its close counterpart, the Mechanised (Tracked) Infantry Battalion is based on the FV432 armoured personnel carrier. In organisational terms the Armoured Infantry

and Mechanised (Tracked) Infantry Battalions are very similar and differ only in the vehicles used by their equivalents of the Rifle Companies, for even in an Armoured Infantry Battalion many of the vehicles used by the Fire Support and Headquarters Companies are still FV432s.

The two forms of tracked battalion operate in West Germany as part of the three armoured divisions of 1 (BR) Corps. In an emergency they would be joined by the Mechanised (Wheeled) Infantry Battalions who are based in the United Kingdom and who would travel to West Germany in their Saxon wheeled armoured personnel carriers during the build-up period that might lead to war. Battalions remaining in the United Kingdom, or moving to the fringes of the NATO areas, rely on trucks as their main

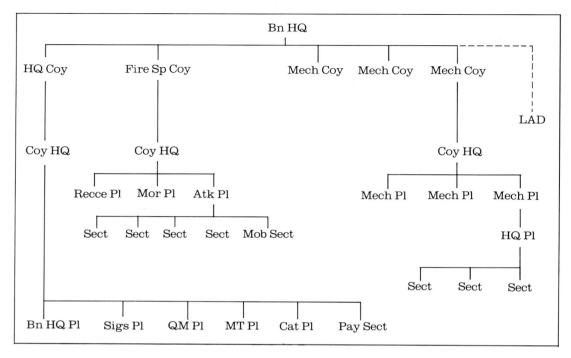

Above:
The structure of a Mechanised (Tracked) Battalion.

mode of transport. The United Kingdom-based battalions are known as Home Defence Infantry Battalions and at one time were referred to as Type B battalions. There are also TA Infantry battalions, some allocated for use by BAOR and some for Home Defence, both of which rely upon unarmoured wheeled transport.

Thus the main difference between the four types of battalion is their mode of transport. They also differ in manpower terms, but as a very rough guide the manpower establishment for the Warrior and FV432 battalions is around 750 officers and men while for the Saxon-based and Home Defence battalions it is somewhat less (around 630 officers and men). In time of war, reserve officers and other personnel will be drafted in to swell these numbers.

Each of the four types of battalion has four main elements — a Battalion Headquarters (Bn HQ), a Headquarters Company (HQ Coy), a Fire Support Company (Fire Sp Coy) and three Rifle Companies (Rifle Coys). In an Armoured Infantry Battalion the latter are

known as Armoured Companies and in the Mechanised (Tracked) Battalions they are Mechanised Companies.

Each battalion also has a Royal Electrical and Mechanical Engineers (REME) Light Aid Detachment (LAD) who keep the vehicles of the battalion serviceable. Their organisation can be described at this point for they have a HQ LAD containing the bulk of the battalion's repair and recovery vehicles, and three LAD Sections — one for each Rifle Company. The LAD Sections have only two repair vehicles each — usually a FV434 REME repair vehicle and a back-up FV432. HQ LAD has more tracked and wheeled repair and recovery vehicles plus a mobile spare parts section based in 4-tonne trucks. In time, the Armoured Infantry Battalion LADs will have seven Warrior ARRVs (armoured repair and recovery vehicles).

The Battalion Headquarters is small — consisting of the Battalion Commander and his immediate staff. They operate a single command vehicle which is usually a specially equipped FV432 or Saxon, although the Armoured Infantry Battalions will use a special command version of Warrior. Operationally they will work with the Battalion Platoon HQ (see below).

HQ Coy is a sizeable organisation in its own right, being the administration and supply unit for the battalion. The Company has its

The 51mm Light Mortar, now on issue as a platoon weapon.
Royal Ordnance

own Company HQ with a Ferret Scout Car (FSC) or Land Rover provided for general liaison with the rest of the battalion. Under the command of this HQ come five platoons and a Pay Section, the latter looking after general financial matters for the rest of the battalion. Their personnel come from the Royal Army Pay Corps (RAPC) and they deal not only with pay but with battalion accounts and money matters generally.

One of the HQ Company is the Battalion HQ Platoon which consists of four sections. They are the Intelligence Section, the Orderly Room, the Provost Section and the Medical Section. These are self-explanatory, but normally the Medical Section consists of a single Royal Army Medical Corps (RAMC) officer. More RAMC personnel would be drafted into the Section in time of war.

The Signals Platoon (Sigs Pl) is found from within the battalion and only in time of war would a single Rear Link Detachment from the Royal Signals (R SIGNALS) be added. The Sigs Pl may also include an ambulance.

The battalion Motor Transport Platoon (MT Pl) provides the vehicles to carry supplies for the rest of the battalion. The bulk of the carrying capacity is provided by 4-tonne and 8-tonne trucks and Stalwart HMLCs (high mobility load carriers), but the Stalwarts are scheduled to be phased out and replaced by more 8-tonners (Bedford

TM 4-4s). Land Rovers are used to carry small loads.

The Quartermaster Platoon (QM Pl) acts as the battalion's main stores administration and holding element, while the Catering Platoon (Cat Pl) is usually split up among the various units of the battalion to provide the cooks from the Army Catering Corps (ACC); there are usually around 20 to a battalion. One further non-Infantry individual attached to the battalion can be mentioned at this point. He is the single instructor from the Army Physical Training Corps (APTC).

The 'teeth' of the Infantry battalion are the three Rifle Companies. Each has its own Company HQ with a small staff and the appropriate vehicles, including a FV432 or Land Rover ambulance. Each Company has three platoons commanded by a junior officer who has his own Platoon Headquarters based on one vehicle. Under his command are three personnel carriers (Warrior, FV432, Saxon or 4-tonne truck, as appropriate), each carrying a section. The size of the Section varies slightly according to the vehicle involved. Warriors and FV432s carry Sections of 10 men (including the driver) while Saxons carry Sections of nine men (again including the driver). Home Defence Battalion Sections have eight men.

Within each Rifle Company one section is trained for the Assault Pioneer (Asslt Pnr)

role. In Home Defence Infantry Battalions the Assault Pioneers come under the command of HQ Coy. The Assault Pioneers carry out virtually all the many and varied combat engineer tasks carried out by the Sappers of the Royal Engineers (RE), and for these the Assault Pioneers are trained by the Sappers. Their duties involve mine laying and clearing. creating or clearing battlefield obstacles, carrying out demolitions, assisting in the preparation of weapon positions or battlefield defences, preparing approach routes for the rest of the battalion, erecting barbed wire or tape barricades, and many other similar tasks. All the above tasks could be carried out by the Combat Engineers of the RE Field Regiments, but in battle they would almost inevitably be heavily involved in major combat engineering operations within the Battle Group so the Infantry battalions are thus able to utilise their Assault Pioneers to tackle all but the heaviest or most difficult of such tasks.

While dealing with special skills, a battalion can have up to four sniper sections with two men in each. They usually answer direct to Bn HQ but may be attached to virtually any part of the battalion and also carry out a second job. Exactly what part and what job is decided by the Battalion Commander. A battalion has at least one Sniper Instructor (trained by the Small Arms School Corps) who trains the rest of the snipers in the battalion.

The Fire Support Company, as its name implies, provides the fire support for the three Rifle Companies. To this end it has its own Company Headquarters and three Platoons, plus the usual REME LAD Section. The Company HQ has a small Training Wing attached to administer the training of the Company and contains the Assault Pioneer Warrant Officer. In time of war this Wing would probably be absorbed into other parts of the battalion.

Under the Fire Support Company HQ come

Far right:
A Spartan fitted with a Milan Compact Turret.

Right:
Soldiers of the Royal Irish Rangers loading an 81mm mortar on a FV432.

the Reconnaissance Platoon (Recce Pl), the Anti-tank Platoon (Atk Pl) and the Mortar Platoon (Mor Pl). The Recce Pl is based on Scimitars in Warrior and FV432 battalions, the Fox in Saxon battalions and Land Rovers in Home Defence battalions. Tracked battalions have a Platoon HQ based on two vehicles and three two-vehicle sections. Wheeled battalions simply have two-vehicle sections — Saxon battalions having four Sections and Home Defence battalions having three.

The Anti-Tank Platoons come in for rather more variation. BAOR battalions have an establishment of 24 Milan FPs (Firing Posts) while Home Defence battalions have only six (TA Infantry Home Defence battalions have no Milans at all). The tracked battalions use FV432s to carry the Milan teams while the wheeled battalions use Land Rovers. In the Warrior and FV432 battalions the Atk Pl has a Platoon HQ with two FV432s and five sections. Four of the sections each have their own Section HQ (Sect HQ) using one FV432 carrying a single FP. Under the Sect HQ are two Detachments (Det) each with a single FV432 carrying two FPs. There is also a Mobile Section (Mob Sect) with four Detach-

ments, each with a single Spartan armed with a Milan Compact Turret (MCT); Mob Sects in Saxon battalions use 1-tonne Land Rovers while the other sections use ¾-tonne Land Rovers.

The Mortar Platoon in tracked battalions has a Pl HQ equipped with two Sultan command vehicles — the only such vehicles in Infantry service. It commands four sections. Each of these sections consists of two detachments, each with a mortar-carrying FV432 and a Mortar Fire Control (MFC) Party in a Spartan. Wheeled battalions carry their mortars on 1-tonne Land Rovers and have ½-tonne Land Rovers for the MFC Party.

As the IW and LSW are issued throughout the Infantry, the GPMGs at present in the rifle companies will be withdrawn and a new GPMG(SF) Platoon will be added to the Fire Support Company.

That completes the detailed outline of the Infantry battalion. There are many minor variations between types of battalion and even individual battalions, and from time to time rearrangements are made to satisfy new issues of equipment or changes in manpower levels.

25

4 The Infantry at Work

In any future conflict, Infantry units will be involved in the All-Arms battle that will follow should the Warsaw Pact nations ever move against the NATO Central Front in Europe. The British contribution to such a conflict would include the Infantry battalions which are part of 1 (BR) Corps and thus partly responsible for the defence of a sector of the North German Plain. The sector extends from a line just north of Hannover down to a line just north of Kassel. The forward defence line is the Inner German Border (IGB), ie the border between the Federal Republic of Germany and the Democratic German Republic.

The soldiers of 1 (BR) Corps will not be fighting alone. They are part of the NATO Northern Army Group (NORTHAG) with, to their north, the West German 1 (GE) Corps and the Belgian 1 (BE) Corps to their south. Air support will be supplied by Royal Air Force Germany (RAFG) and other air forces from NATO's Second Tactical Air Force (2 ATAF).

The Infantry in 1 (BR) Corps are thus only an increment of NATO's armed forces that stand ready to deter aggression. Within 1 (BR) Corps they are an important force for the Infantry contributes 16 battalions. At the time of writing the Warrior infantry combat vehicle had yet to be issued so these battalions were still largely based on the use of the FV432 armoured personnel carrier and the Saxon wheeled armoured personnel carrier. Of these two the FV432 was by far the most numerous and is still used to equip the battalions that are actually located in West Germany, so the way these Mechanised (Tracked) Battalions operate is worthy of consideration in some detail. (For the record, Saxon battalions operate in the same manner as that outlined below.)

Below:
Infantry debussing from a Warrior APC.
School of Infantry

The role of the mechanised (tracked) battalions may be stated as: 'To hold ground which provides freedom of movement for the Armour, to fight at close quarters on the one hand and to destroy enemy armour at medium and close range on the other.

This statement varies somewhat from the previously-quoted definition of 'To close with an enemy and destroy his will and ability to fight', mainly because within 1 (BR) Corps the Infantry will be fighting in close partnership with armour, artillery and combat engineers. That basic Infantry role will still be present but within 1 (BR) Corps

Above:
A FV432 fitted with a L37 turret.

the Infantry operates as a powerful partner as part of a team, all with the same objective of destroying the enemy. In particular the Infantry work very closely with the tanks of the Royal Armoured Corps (RAC) and with the fire support of the Royal Artillery (RA). Further close support comes from the Sappers of the Regiments of the Royal Engineers (RE). In fact these Arms work together so closely that they formed into what are termed as Battle Groups. The exact size and form of a Battle Group will vary according to the size of the combat task involved. As stated elsewhere in this book, some Battle Groups will be heavy in Infantry and light in armour while others might well be the reverse. Battle Groups may thus be Armoured or Infantry according to their most important component and how they are commanded. Within the Battle Group various company or squadron groups will be formed as required but the entire system is flexible and can be regrouped and rearranged as the tactical situation dictates.

The need for the Battle Group has been determined by the realisation that during modern warfare no particular Arm can operate in splendid isolation. Tanks by themselves cannot attack defensive positions (except under very special circumstances) or

operate in close or built-up terrain, while the Artillery cannot take or occupy ground. In their turn the Infantry cannot operate without the fire support provided by both Artillery and Armour. All three of these Arms require the support that can only be provided by combat engineers while they, in their turn, need the protection and fire support of the other Arms to carry out their widely varied battlefield tasks. The modern battle is thus an All-Arms battle that is conducted in mutual and close co-operation at all levels of command. The Battle Group is the physical manifestation of this co-operation.

Within the Battle Group the FV432 is the Infantry's main vehicle. It is an armoured personnel carrier that merely provides mobility and protection for an Infantry section on a battlefield. While the FV432's tracks impart a high degree of cross-country mobility, the

Above:
A Scimitar operating alongside a Chieftain tank.

Below:
Milan crews about to board their 1-tonne Land Rover.

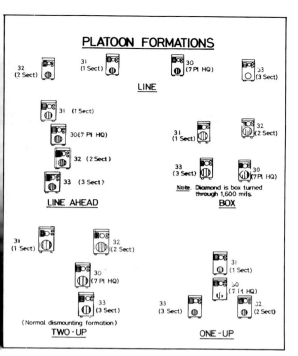

A few of the various platoon formations used by Mechanised Infantry (Tracked) Battalions.

guided or unguided missile. Thus at any time the FV432 commander, who is also the Section Commander, has to consider that his entire section could be knocked out by a single hit from an anti-armour weapon. This alone dictates many of the tactics that mechanised Infantry have to adopt.

In the attack the Infantry have to dismount to fight. They cannot fight from their vehicles for the basic reason that they have no means to use their weapons from inside the vehicle and anyway, even if they could they would still not be able to use that important Infantry asset, ground.

Ground for the Infantry is a combat medium. They have to use ground to close with an enemy, occupy ground to deny its use to an enemy and hold ground to allow other Arms to move. They cannot do any of these from within the confines of the FV432 interior. Therefore they have to dismount to achieve their objectives and at such times the FV432 is at best limited to providing supporting fire. It therefore has to be either removed from the scene of action or placed where it can be protected from enemy retaliation.

term 'protection' is relative as its armour is light and proof only against light artillery splinters and small arms fire. It is also lightly armed, having only a single 7.62mm machine gun for self-protection, but there are two types of mounting for this weapon. One is an open pintle next to the commander's cupola while the other is a small one-man turret. Both types are used by the Infantry, usually at a ratio of two pintle guns and two turret guns to every platoon, although in some battalions more turret guns might be available. The turret mounting means that the gun can be fired without the gunner having to leave the protection of the vehicle's armour, allowing the weapon to be used to provide close supporting fire both in attack and defence. This capability does not transform the FV432 into a mechanised combat vehicle for it is far too lightly armoured for that; nor does it have the necessary fire-power.

The light armour of the FV432 means that it is also highly vulnerable to all anti-armour weapons, be they high-velocity gun projectiles or the various forms of anti-tank

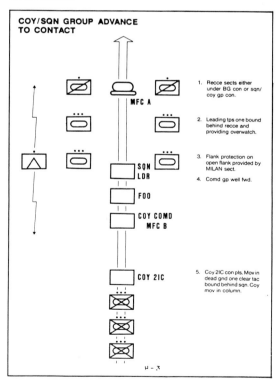

A typical formation of a company/squadron Battle Group advancing to contact.

29

Right:
A soldier standing guard armed with the SA80 Individual Weapon and LAW 80.
Hunting Engineering

Far right:
Challenger (seen here) or Chieftain main battle tanks provide intimate support for mechanised and armoured infantry units during the final stages of any attack.

The vulnerability of the FV432 dictates the tactics used by the Infantry in several ways but it must be stressed that this vulnerability is relative. Any armour, no matter how light, is better than nothing on a battlefield and the FV432 also provides many other advantages for the foot soldier. The most important is mobility, not only in simply getting around from place to place but being able to charge towards an enemy position and reinforce the shock impact of an attack by the sheer momentum produced by speed of movement. In addition, this mobility keeps soldiers fresh and less tired than would otherwise be the case when sheer foot-slogging is the alternative, and the vehicle also acts as a carrier for all the bits and pieces that support and keep the soldier in action. This includes extra ammunition, ration packs, water (not forgetting the invaluable water boiler that every FV432 carries), spare clothing, personal effects, digging tools, NBC clothing and so on. If these items were not loaded on the FV432 they would have to be either carried by the soldiers themselves or on unprotected trucks with their limited cross country mobility with all its attendant disadvantages. Other advantages of the FV432 are that they can be NBC sealed to allow their occupants to survive in otherwise hostile environments and they can carry radios with a greater power and range than smaller back-pack equipments. Last but not least, the FV432's armour enables the Infantry to move forward close to the safety limits imposed by the supporting artillery fire, enabling the Infantry to move really close to their objectives before having to debus.

For the moment, Warrior is still in the future so to consider exactly how a FV432 section is employed in action we will consider a typical attack scenario. In so doing we will be able to consider some of the tactical considerations and decisions that have to be taken in any mechanised Infantry action and outline some of the drills that have to become routine to trained soldiers. We will also consider not a full Battle Group, but the actions of a smaller formation, the Squadron/Company Group. As its title implies this is a Group formed from a squadron of tanks and an Infantry company.

In any period prior to action a great deal of time has to be taken up in the sheer mechanics of preparation. Vehicles and their radios have to be serviced and checked to ensure that they are fully serviceable and only then are they loaded with fuel, ammunition, ration packs and other supplies. There is a carefully laid down loading procedure for the FV432 to make sure that everything is in its place and accessible when needed. Both interior and exterior racks and stowage locations have to be carefully loaded and lashed down. All these loading procedures are practised constantly during training. Once loaded, each vehicle carries sufficient supplies to keep the Section in

action for up to 48hr — only extra fuel will be required during that period.

Once loaded with supplies, the FV432 is then loaded with men. Once again each man has his own personal check-out list including items such as weapon checks, personal ammunition allotments, combat dressings, full webbing and other equipment stowage, and so on. Back-pack radios are checked and so are all the 101 other details that are gone over time and again during repeated training. When all is ready the vehicle commanders are briefed and then it is time for the off.

FV432 can travel long distances on their own tracks which is just as well for there will be no spare tank transporters to help them on their way. Whenever possible, at least during the early stages of the journey to the combat zone, the vehicles stick to the roads to maintain a good travelling speed but all the time they have to keep about 50 metres behind the vehicle in front to avoid presenting a tempting target to low-flying enemy strike aircraft. At any halt vehicles leave the road and should space themselves about 20 to 25 metres apart for the same reason. Any vehicle that breaks down has to leave the route and hoist a yellow breakdown flag to attract the REME LAD as it passes.

When the combat area is reached the FV432s leave the roads and assume combat formations. For the FV432s these can take several forms according to the tactical situation but one of the most commonly used is the Box, together with its close variant the Diamond. Both are easy to assume and control and both can be readily altered into other formations when necessary. During any halt each vehicle will attempt to take cover under foliage or erect camouflage netting screens to avoid detection.

Prior to an attack the FV432 section has to form up with the rest of the Group in an assembly area. For our scenario we will assume the Group is based around part of a squadron of Challenger tanks and a single Mechanised (Tracked) Infantry Company. Available for support are a battery of 155mm M109A2 self-propelled howitzers and a troop of armoured engineers mounted in Chieftain AVREs (Armoured Vehicle Royal Engineers) plus a RE Field Troop.

While still in the assembly area the Group Commander is allotted a combat task, in this case an attack on an enemy force that has run out of steam following a penetration of our forward defence positions. Although small in numbers (about one company plus some light armour) such a position can be turned into a bridgehead for further expansion so it has to be eliminated. From this point onwards the Group starts to employ a series of what should be routine procedures.

One of these operations is the establishment of certain criteria such as when, exactly where and along what lines (ie from what direction) the attack will be pressed home.

Certain measures to ensure close control have to be established, such as the axis of advance, the boundaries of the operation (to prevent interference with other operations and vice versa), lines to report progress and assist navigation, and bound lines to mark the various stages of the operation along which progress may be halted to make fresh progress assessments and to regroup prior to the final attack. All these controls are established, named (usually with nicknames and numbers) and broadcast over the command radio nets.

Before any move the various formations have to sort themselves out and get into formation and position. During a standard advance to contact the Group will form up into three main formations. First will be the Command Group spread evenly on either side of the axis of advance. Well forward and to the flanks will be two Recce Sections. Behind them come four Challenger troops, again left and right of the axis with the Mortar Fire Control (MFC) Party well forward in their

Spartan ready to call up support fire. Also up with the lead tanks is the main Command Group proper with the Challenger Squadron commander, the Mechanised Infantry Company commander and the Gunner Forward Observation Officer (FOO) in his FV432. They may be accompanied by a section of Milan-carrying Spartans with MCTs but normally these are held in reserve.

Behind them come the three Mechanised Infantry Platoons and the Company 2 IC (Second-in-Command). The distance between these two main elements will vary according to the type of terrain and the nature of the expected threat. In the open country the intervals will be greater than those in close or built-up country, In really close country the order might well be reversed with the Infantry on foot along with or in front of the tanks. Tanks cannot operate safely in wooded or built-up terrain for the threat from enemy anti-tank teams is too great and anyway their ability to use their main weapons to the full will be reduced. Under such circumstances the Infantry will have to clear the way and if the anti-armour risk is high they have to dismount from their FV432s and operate on foot.

In our scenario the terrain is open so the tanks are forward, the FV432s following and

Below:
A long-range shot of an Infantry platoon advancing with Chieftain tanks in close support.

in the third element, the tail, come the ambulances and the LAD. Further back still are the A1 Echelon waiting to bring forward combat supplies such as ammunition and fuel when called for.

As the Recce Section arrives close to the objective it reports back to the Command Group and the Challengers move forward to take up hull-down positions before they positively identify the enemy and engage him. The Command Group then move forward to make their own appreciation of the situation and together work out exactly what they will do next.

Once the appreciation is finished the orders go back to the platoons that have followed the advance but are by then waiting in dead ground or behind cover some way from the enemy positions. The orders from the Command Group follow an established pattern and are made in a form that can be heard by all involved within the Squadron/Company Group so they can understand what is going on even if any particular item does not actively involve them. One of the prime points in this command sequence is the establishment of a start line and time, and from these the various sub-unit commanders can make their own arrangements and issue their own orders.

The usual formation the actual form-up for an attack will take is the placing of a Fire Support Group of Challengers and mortars away to a flank from where they can lay down their fire. More support fire will be supplied by the M109A2 battery that could be located some thousands of metres away. In our case no air support is available or required, and for once the combat engineers have no precise task.

Two Challenger troops form up one on either flank of the start line while a single Challenger forms up in front of each of the two mechanised platoons involved to provide what is termed as intimate support. The third Infantry platoon is kept slightly to the rear as a reserve and can link up with a third Challenger from the intimate support troop when necessary. The Company Commander places himself at the most tactically advantageous point. The entire start line position is guarded by dismounted Milans and sometimes by Recce Platoon Scimitars.

When the time comes to move the two Challenger troops move to a position 50m or so each side of the objective and deliver suppressive fire. The Artillery and the mortars both supply covering and suppressive fire directly on to the objective and the Infantry platoons move forward at speed, each covered by their own intimate support Challenger.

As the FV432s move towards the objective they do so under a supporting hail of artillery, mortar and tank gun fire. As they close the FV432 turret machine guns can join in but eventually the time comes for the sections to debus and make the final attack on foot. During this stage the individual FV432 commanders and drivers are virtually following the herd but they do so in a predetermined formation and they follow well-instilled battle drills that dictate section formations and actions. Inside each FV432 weapons are given their final check, bayonets are fixed, back-pack radios are switched on and the rear door is unclamped.

The actual point at which the debus will be made depends on many factors. Too far forward and the FV432s will be very vulnerable to any anti-armour weapons that could well knock out entire sections while they are still in their vehicles. Too far back and the Infantry will have to move forward on foot for distances that will slow them down and reduce the impact of the attack; they will also be vulnerable to enemy fire for longer periods. The ideal debus point is in dead ground and out of sight and reach of the enemy's short range weapons, but such happy occasions will be few. In many circumstances obstacles or the very nature of the terrain will often dictate the point at which the Infantry will have to dismount. In any instance there is no replacement for careful reconnaissance and the gathering of information relating to likely debus positions from as many sources as possible — if time is available.

While the final stages of the approach to the debus point are being made, the individual FV432 sections have little idea of what is going on outside their vehicles. Although the various orders have been broadcast over the internal vehicle intercoms, the individual soldiers have no idea of what the outside world looks like or what is actually happening for they have no vision ports at their disposal. The first they see of the outside world is when the Section Commander gives the order to debus and the vehicle lurches to a halt.

This initial period as the Infantry debus is one of the most awkward moments of any Infantry operation. For a brief period as he leaves the FV432 the individual soldier has to orientate himself and associate himself with his immediate surroundings, but this disad-

COY/SQN GP QUICK

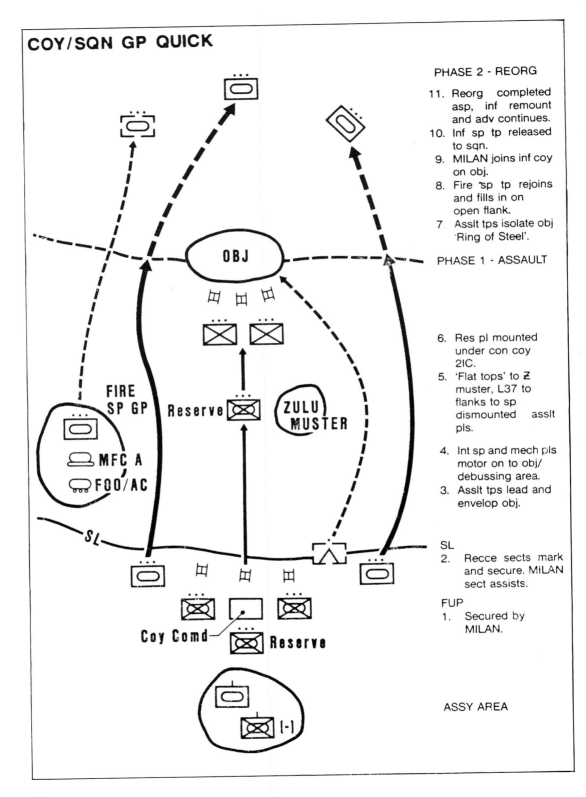

PHASE 2 - REORG

11. Reorg completed asp, inf remount and adv continues.
10. Inf sp tp released to sqn.
9. MILAN joins inf coy on obj.
8. Fire sp tp rejoins and fills in on open flank.
7. Asslt tps isolate obj 'Ring of Steel'.

PHASE 1 - ASSAULT

6. Res pl mounted under con coy 2IC.
5. 'Flat tops' to Z muster, L37 to flanks to sp dismounted asslt pls.
4. Int sp and mech pls motor on to obj/debussing area.
3. Asslt tps lead and envelop obj.

SL
2. Recce sects mark and secure. MILAN sect assists.

FUP
1. Secured by MILAN.

ASSY AREA

Left:
The stages of a quick attack carried out by a small Battle Group.

vantage is overcome by a dismounting drill that is repeated time and time again until it becomes an automatic reaction.

The FV432 halts with the hull front facing the enemy. The first soldier out opens the rear door and stands there holding it open as the rest dismount; he could also assist the radio man by erecting the back-pack radio aerial as he leaves and he closes the door again as the last man leaves the FV432. Each soldier moves to the flank on the side of the vehicle on which he was seated, taking up a fire position about 20m to one side and about 5m in front of the FV432. The Section commander is one of the last out, leaving through the rear door.

The Section thus forms two Fire Teams, each formed from three riflemen and one Light Support Weapon (LSW). One of the riflemen in each section might also carry a LAW 80, but if no immediate armour threat is anticipated this might well be left in the FV432. In any case the final stages of the attack are covered by the intimate support Challengers.

There will be a few occasions when the FV432 will be able to remain in its debus position and deliver covering fire from its turret gun. The usual procedure is a rapid turn and a drive away to the rear to a preselected position known as a Zulu Muster. There the empty FV432s are taken in hand and any opportunity to use their machine guns from safe positions will be taken.

Back on the objective the Infantry sections will have to fight their way through the objective in time-honoured style. At an opportune moment the reserve platoon might enter the fray. All the time the intimate support Challengers will be close by, using their 120mm main guns and co-axial machine guns to knock out enemy positions and weapons while away to the flanks the other Challenger troops will be covering the flanks and rear of the objective to keep enemy armour at bay; this latter operation is known rather dramatically as the 'ring of steel'.

Once the objective has been taken the next stage is to form up again ready to beat off any counter-attack. The Fire Support Group will move forward to a flank position and Milan teams will take up positions on and around the objective. If the position is to be defended

for any length of time the main defensive weapon will be Milan with machine guns carefully sited to support them. If time allows the Assault Pioneers will lay defensive anti-tank minefields (with a fair scattering of anti-personnel mines to deter enemy mine-clearing teams) and the Sappers could use their plant to produce vehicle slots into which FV432s with turret machine guns could be inserted to provide extra defensive fire. The Gunners will provide their defensive fire plans.

If all is well it is then time for the tail to move forward and for the ambulances to pick up casualties; the LAD will do the same for the vehicles. The A1 Echelon will move forward to carry out resupply operations. The general rearrangements such as the support Challengers moving back to their squadron will take place and the Artillery FOO will consider his next priorities.

For the Infantry Sections it will probably mean a period of digging in to stand ready with LAW 80s close at hand and prepared for any enemy counter-moves. It could also mean the sending forward of the FV432s from the Zulu Muster ready for another stage of an advance or a move to another combat task.

The success of any operation such as the above depends on several factors. High on the list must come the close co-operation between all the Arms involved, the establishment of clearly understood objectives and operating methods, and the issuing of clear and precise orders and briefings. Once the actual operation commences the Squadron/Company Group and its various constituents can then follow well-established and practised battle drills.

The above scenario has outlined the various stages of an advance to contact and a Squadron/Company Group quick attack. They are only two forms of action that a similar group or a Battle Group might expect to undertake, others being the withdrawal from contact, the ambush, the counter-attack, actions in support of a nuclear strike, fighting in built-up areas (FIBUA) and so forth. All require constant training and rehearsal to the point where all the various actions become almost second nature.

When Warrior arrives on the scene the vehicle protection factor will be improved but the Warrior's armour is still relatively light. Improvements which will be made over FV432 mainly concern the armament. Warrior is a true mechanised infantry combat vehicle armed with a 30mm Rarden Gun and a 7.62mm Chain Gun to provide the Infantry

35

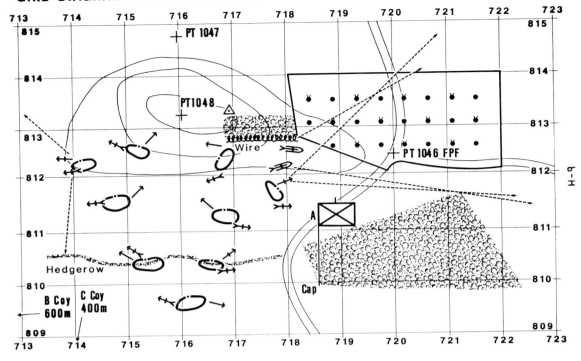

Above:
Diagrammatic layout of an Infantry company in a defensive position.

with the ability to produce increased amounts of supporting fire and the capability to knock out enemy armoured personnel carriers and light reconnaissance vehicles. Warrior also has improved mobility that will enable it to keep pace with supporting armour. The Infantry will still have to dismount from the Warrior to fight, but, in addition to the two dismounted fire teams, Warrior will also be able to supply direct supporting fire from its turret weapons. In addition the Warrior could also be employed to act as a forward or flank screening vehicle for fixed positions.

Perhaps the most important factor regarding Warrior is the increased fire-power it will enable the Infantry to provide at any particular point in an action. Three men are required to fight Warrior; the commander, driver and gunner. That leaves only seven men able to dismount and form the two Fire Teams. This reduction in Fire Team manpower will be more than off-set by the increase in fire-power possible with SA80 and the extra supporting fire from the Warrior turret weapons. However it is unlikely that any particular section can expect prolonged support from its own individual Warrior. It is expected that whenever possible 'empty' Warriors will be organised into mobile Fire Teams that can be much more versatile and effective collectively than vehicles operating in isolation.

One thing is for certain. Any Infantry action will be an involved, noisy and dangerous affair. The amount of enemy and friendly fire flying about, with all the horrendous noise of artillery, tank guns and mortar bombs, will be of an order that would make any unprepared individual simply want to crawl into a hole and stay there until it is all over. The trained soldier has no such recourse for he has to leave the cover of his familiar and relatively comfortable FV432, advance on foot into enemy fire and destroy his enemy at the traditional close quarters. That takes something special, something that cannot come from training alone. It takes leadership, quiet and determined courage and an aggressive spirit, all of which are well evident in the modern Infantry.

5 The Infantry in Northern Ireland

The current troubles in Northern Ireland have been in progress for so long now that they have come to be virtually accepted as part of the British Army's way of life. As always, the Infantry has to bear the brunt of the workload involved and over the years has borne the larger proportion of the casualties that have been inflicted from both sides of the Irish social and political divide. In return, the Infantry has acquired invaluable skills at many levels, resulting in an enviable reputation among other armed forces as a highly efficient counter-insurgency and internal security force.

The Army was called upon to assist local security forces to reimpose law and order during 1969 when open insurrection and rioting against the established authorities broke out on such a scale that the local security agencies were overwhelmed. At first the arrival of soldiers was regarded as a welcome relief by many but within weeks the peculiar nature of Northern Irish social and political life meant that Army uniforms were no longer welcome on the streets and the Army itself became a target. During the uproar of that period it was not universally recognised that the Army was not acting on its own authority, although for a short period it had to take on responsibilities that were normally those of the local police forces. The Army had to operate under the direction and auspices of the local authorities, and that fact has not changed. Another fact not always understood during those early days, and especially during 1969, was that the Army was neither properly equipped nor trained for the type of operation in which it found itself involved. Although training regarding 'Duties in Support of a Civil Power' had for long been part of any military education, the routines and measures involved had always been regarded as relating to colonial situations and were not always high on most training course priorities.

Not surprisingly then, during those early days the Army often found itself making mistakes that all too often made a bad situation worse. Far from the unrest being quelled, the Province of Ulster entered a period when riots, killings, bombings and intimidation became the virtual norm. No part of Northern Ireland seemed to escape as the frustrations and quarrels (real and imagined) of generations worked themselves out in the towns and villages of Ulster. The Army, and the Infantry in particular, did what they could but the Troubles continued on such a scale that at one time over 22,000 soldiers were on duty in Northern Ireland to assist the local security forces in attempting to keep the Queen's Peace.

Over the years since 1969 the Troubles have followed a pattern — settling down to reasonably manageable levels only to break out all over again whenever it suited troublemakers on one side or the other. Consequently, soldiers found themselves spending time on repeated 'Operation Banner' roulement tours that involved periods of four months away from their real purpose plus even more time preparing for those tours and winding down again afterwards. It was and still is hard and mainly unrewarding work, with the ever-present danger of the terrorist bomb or gun and all too often with the local population apathetic, if not downright hostile, to the Army's activities and presence.

Recent years have seen a considerable scaling down of the terrorist activities of the

early and mid-1970s. Ulster is still a place where terrorists do their best to keep their operations in the forefront of public awareness and where the security forces are still the target of their lethal activities, but generally speaking things have quietened down considerably. The Army now has only six Infantry battalions resident in the Province with a further two on roulement tours at any one time (one from BAOR plus one from the United Kingdom; their tours now last 4½ months). The Army population is about 9,000 regular soldiers plus 6,500 or so from the Ulster Defence Regiment (UDR). The vast bulk of peace-keeping tasks have now been assumed by the Royal Ulster Constabulary (RUC) with the support of the UDR who are themselves very much part of the British Army and who are often commanded or trained by Infantry officers and personnel.

Much of the credit for the gradual reduction in levels of violence must go to the Infantry. Over the years they have been the main increment of the Army's contribution to keeping the peace in Ulster and it is their dedication and training for the task that has done so much to achieve the present situation.

After the initial events of 1969, and once the scale and long-term implications of the Army's role in Ulster were appreciated, there began a programme of training at all levels that has made the Army, and the Infantry in particular, into one of the finest counter-insurgency forces in the world. The results have been such that although there is no end in sight to the present levels of terrorist activity, they have been contained throughout much of Northern Ireland and the Regular Army no longer has any on-going commitment in well over 85% of the Province.

This has been achieved at a considerable cost. The number of civilians killed runs into thousands and the Army has suffered well over 400 deaths, including those from the UDR. Many more have been wounded and yet more have been scarred mentally by what they have seen and experienced.

At the time of writing the Army in Northern Ireland was organised into three United Kingdom Land Forces (UKLF) Brig-

Far left:
Men of the Black Watch prepare for a patrol in Northern Ireland in 1977.
MoD

Left:
On duty at a Vehicle Check Point (VCP) on the Border.
HQ Northern Ireland Public Relations

ades under the command of HQ Northern Ireland at Lisburn. No 8 Infantry Brigade is based at Londonderry, No 39 Infantry Brigade at Lisburn and No 3 Infantry Brigade at Armagh. No 8 Infantry Brigade has four resident battalions at Londonderry, Ballykelly, Omagh and Aldergrove. No 39 Infantry Brigade has two resident battalions at Hollywood and Ballykinler and two roulement battalions, one in Armagh and the other based on the Springfield Road in Belfast. No 3 Infantry Brigade is headquartered at Drummodd Barracks in Armagh and is primarily responsible for border security. It takes its manpower from the other two brigades.

The eight battalions are located to provide support to the local security forces in the three main areas of continuing unrest, namely Londonderry, West Belfast and the 'bandit country' along the borders of South Armagh and Fermanagh. Throughout the rest of the Province the RUC and UDR rarely have to call upon the Army for support. They have their local situations well under control and scale their activities accordingly.

The security forces, including the Army, operate within what are known as Tactical Areas of Responsibility (TAORs). Each TAOR roughly coincides with the RUC's organisational boundaries and is sub-divided into smaller regions which are gradually divided down further into areas which can be patrolled by the smallest Army unit operating within Northern Ireland, the four-man 'brick'. Each brick consists of a Junior NCO and three soldiers. The number of 'bricks' in any particular area is varied according to the terrain, the level of unlawful activity, the operations in progress and other factors. Each man within the 'brick' is responsible for keeping guard over all other members of the 'brick' so at any one instant all-round observation is carried out and any movements are made with at least one man ready to provide covering fire.

The bulk of the routine work carried out by the Infantry in Ulster is patrolling. Operating in all weathers, most patrols are carried out on foot, although in potentially dangerous rural areas armoured Land Rovers known as 'Piglets' are used, while in the cities patrols use ageing 'Pigs', ie Humber wheeled armoured personnel carriers, many

dating from the mid-1950s. At times helicopters are provided to insert patrols into
remote areas. The constant patrolling has
two main objectives. One is to keep terrorists
uncertain of where the security forces might
next apppear and thus keep them off balance.
The other is to reassure the law-abiding
populace by their very presence.

Another major activity is the manning and
operation of vehicle check points (VCPs) to
keep an eye on traffic and search vehicles for
unlawful contents. The simple maintenance
of VCPs ensures that terrorists cannot move
men or weapons around with impunity and
therefore have to utilise other and more
difficult methods to operate. The searching of
premises or open country is another constant
activity — a usually boring and unrewarding
task that is only rarely greeted with success
by unprompted arms finds or the discovery of
explosives caches. Even more time-
consuming are the various forms of overt and
covert surveillance operations carried out
along the border areas or in some urban
locations.

It should be restressed that in Northern
Ireland the Army cannnot operate auton-
omously. Its activities are severely proscribed
and even in times of danger soldiers are often
placed at a disadvantage by being unable to
open or return fire except under carefully
restricted circumstances. They have to operate under the control and guidance of the

RUC and the local civic authorities, for they
are the official bodies who retain the prime
responsibility to uphold the law. To this end
RUC personnel often patrol alongside the
Army. Many Infantry counter-terrorist operations are commanded by UDR personnel,
usually from the Permanent Cadre (PC) UDR
Companies. Over the years the UDR has
gained considerable internal security expertise to the point where they are now probably
the best internal security force in existence.
Naturally enough the rest of the Army uses
their experience and local knowledge to the
full.

For most Northern Ireland operations the
Infantry carry their normal weapons, with
the L1A1 rifle or IW being the most used —
there is usually little place for machine guns
during counter-insurgency operations, and
if any are required they are usually L4A4
Bren guns. Although the Army is now rarely
involved in riot control situations, the main
munitions used are CS grenades, baton
rounds and the L67A1 riot gun. Armoured
Land Rovers and the venerable 'Pigs' are used
as personnel carriers as they do not have the
emotive appearance of most other armoured
military vehicles which are often classified in
civilian eyes as 'tanks'. Personal protection is
provided by special helmets and sometimes
body armour. Other riot control equipment
includes shields, padded gloves, batons and
leg protectors.

The Army, and the Infantry in particular, still suffer casualties in Northern Ireland for the terrorist will always have the initiative in any internal security situation. Even so, direct attacks upon the Army by terrorists are attempted very rarely nowadays. They have learnt the hard way that the levels of expertise now held by the Army are such that any terrorist attempting anything will usually come off the worst. Instead, resort is now made to booby traps, culvert bombs, sniping or home-made mortar ambushes and the assassination of off-duty security personnel. In towns the main activity is destroying property by bombing.

The main problem for the security forces after nearly 20 years in Ulster is that the terrorists still operating are now a determined, hardened and experienced group. Any operations they attempt are more certain to result in casualties or damage than was once the case. To counter this situation the security forces are usually able to contain terrorist activity within certain limits which it is now rare for any form of unlawful activity to exceed. From time to time 'anniversaries' or similar occurrences result in disturbances but as the years go by the overall levels of violence are gradually being reduced.

Much of the credit for this state of affairs must go to the UDR and RUC who now shoulder the peace-keeping burden in well over 85% of the Province. It has already been mentioned that credit must also go to the dogged patience and hard work of the Infantry who have endured much during the current Troubles. In return they have been provided with new levels of abilities and skills, and a sense of purpose that has kept them going. Above all it has provided the Infantry Junior NCO with an experience of leadership and responsibility that far outweighs anything he could achieve in normal soldiering under peacetime conditions — something that the Infantry will find invaluable in the years ahead.

6 Keeping in Touch

Within the battalion the Infantry provide their own radio communications. They have their own radio networks and they use and maintain their own communications equipments. For support and assistance they can call upon the Royal Signals (R SIGNALS) but the only integral R SIGNALS personnel within the Infantry battalion are a Rear Link Party who would join the battalion only in time of war. They would then form part of the Signals Platoon in the HQ Company.

Every part of the Army relies heavily on radio communications and the Infantry are no less reliant on their internal links than any other Arm. The forms that the links can take are many and vary in range and capability depending on the power and form of the sets involved. Every armoured vehicle within the Infantry battalion has some form of radio link with other vehicles within its own particular unit while others have links to higher command levels or other parts of the battalion. Command vehicles in particular can be expected to be equipped with extra and more powerful equipments. At the lowest communication level are the small man-pack radios with relatively limited ranges.

Today the Infantry is almost entirely equipped with the Clansman series of radio equipments. Some TA Infantry battalions continue to use the older Larkspur or similar systems. Compared to the Larkspur equipments, which belong to an earlier technological generation, Clansman equipments are smaller, lighter, more rugged and are built to very high standards of quality control. They nearly all use some form of rechargeable batteries (that are costly enough items by themselves) and many have special features such as automatic encryption devices, 'whisper' voice input modes and self-tuning aerials. By the use of various 'add-on' units the capabilities of many sets can be extended or improved performance can be obtained.

Listed below are the basic specifications for some of the more widely-used Infantry communication equipments. A full listing of all likely equipments is not possible for security reasons.

Manpack Sets

PRC-344

Frequencies:	225-399.95MHz
Channels:	3,500
RF Power:	2.5W
Approx range (ground to ground):	up to 8km
Approx range (ground to air):	up to 160km at 2,700m altitude
Weight:	7.6kg
Features:	auto rebroadcast, remote and beacon

PRC-349

Frequencies:	37-46.975MHz
Channels:	399 at 25MHz spacing
RF Power:	0.5W
Approx range:	up to 2km
Weight:	2kg
Features:	whisper or loud modes, confidence check

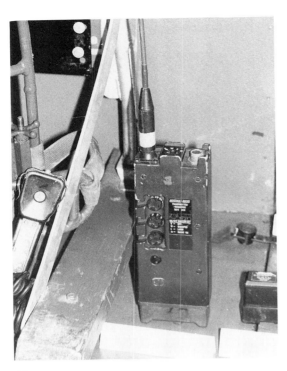

PRC-350

Frequencies:	36-56.975MHz
Channels:	840 at 25MHz spacing
RF Power:	2W
Approx range:	up to 5km with 1.2m whip aerial
Weight:	3.6kg
Features:	whisper and loud modes, confidence check

PRC-351

Frequencies:	30-75.975MHz
Channels:	1,840 at 25MHz spacing
RF Power:	5W
Approx range:	up to 8km with 1.2m whip aerial
Weight:	8.2kg
Features:	auto rebroadcast, remote up to 3km, intercom and call, whisper and loud modes

Above:
The PRC 349 portable transceiver.

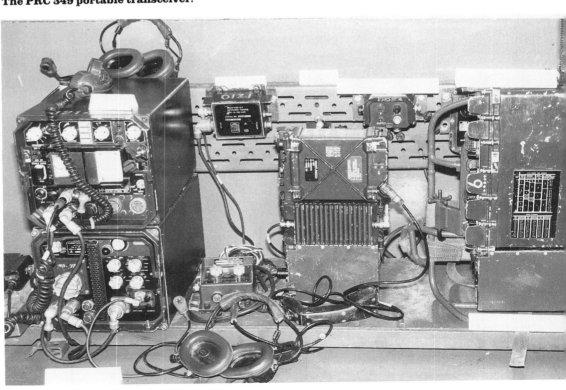

PRC-352

Frequencies:	30-75.975MHz
Channels:	1,840 at 25MHz spacing
RF Power:	up to 20W with amplifier
Range as ground set:	up to 16km
Range as vehicle set:	up to 28km
Weight:	11.4kg
Features:	auto rebroadcast, remote up to 3km, intercom and call, whisper and loud modes

Vehicle Set

VRC-353

Frequencies:	30-75.975MHz
Channels:	1,840 at 25MHz spacing
RF Power:	0.1-50W
Approx range:	up to 30km with 2m whip aerial
Weight:	88kg with battery
Features:	4 power outputs, teleprinter and computer access, auto antenna tuning

Far left, bottom:
A PRC 353 (left) with a PRC 320 high frequency (HF) radio (right).

Left:
The PRC 351 (left) and PRC 352 (right).

Bottom left:
The PRC 344.

7 The School of Infantry

The School of Infantry (SCHINF) is head-quartered at Warminster in Wiltshire, on the western fringe of Salisbury Plain. It is an establishment that can trace its origins back to the formation of the School of Musketry at Hythe in 1854. Since those early days it has expanded considerably to the point where it now has a presence in several parts of the United Kingdom. The School is an establishment where many cap badges will be encountered, not all of them from the Infantry, as will be explained.

The role of the SCHINF is easily stated. It is 'To train selected infantrymen, instructors and commanders from all Arms and Services, up to the rank of Brigadier, in skill-at-arms, support weapons, communications and combined arms tactics.'

To concentrate on the Infantry alone it is instructive to recall that the SCHINF is therefore responsible for the overall training and training standards of the Army's 99 Infantry battalions (including the TA and UDR battalions) and, to put matters further into context, that the Infantry forms 43.5% of the Army's 'teeth' arms. The SCHINF therefore has a considerable responsibility which it carries out in several ways.

One is that it provides the general operating principles for the Infantry in any of the theatres in which they might find themselves. It constantly reviews the overall tactical background within those theatres — not only in a purely parochial Infantry sense, but also in the sense of an All-Arms battle. The Infantry are therefore taught how to operate and liaise with the rest of the Army, for once again it must be stressed that the Infantry now operate as only one combat component within the All-Arms battle. Soldiers are therefore taught how to adapt, think and how to come up with the swift reaction that any situation might require. The SCHINF, as with any similar establishment, cannot hope to train soldiers to meet every possible contingency but it can train them to handle potential problems and difficult situations as they arise.

Warminster and the SCHINF provides a base for the Director of Infantry and is the home of three SCHINF Wings — the Tactics Wing, the Small Arms Wing and the Signals Wing. Also attached to the School is the Junior Division of the Staff College. Under SCHINF at Warminster comes the bulk of a complete Demonstration Battalion of Infantry and a Demonstration Squadron from the Royal Armoured Corps (RAC). The Support Regiment of the nearby Royal School of Artillery (RSA) provides a Demonstration Battery when requested while the SCHINF also has its own Support Unit to provide the usual administration and transport. Further support for the SCHINF at Warminster and Netheravon comes from 27 District Workshop, Royal Electrical and Mechanical Engineers (REME).

Away from Warminster, its nearest wing in geographical terms is the Support Weapons Wing at Netheravon which deals with all support weapons such as Milan, mortars, and the GPMG(SF); not surprisingly the Support Company of the SCHINF Demonstration Battalion resides there. There is a NCOs Tactical Wing at Brecon, together with an associated Gurkha Demonstration Company. SCHINF also has two Training Advisory Groups (TAGs) that are based at Strensall (North) and Aldershot (South) — the TAGs are primarily concerned with providing skill-at-arms courses for the Section Commanders Battle Course (SCBC —

see below) but can have other training roles. Also under SCHINF comes the specialised Northern Ireland Training Advisory Team (United Kingdom Land Forces), or NITAT (UKLF), based at Lydd in Kent.

To return to Warminster, the roles of the three resident Wings are fairly evident from their titles. However the SCHINF also has a 'think tank' function that is not so evident at first, but one which soon becomes apparent when any time is spent there. SCHINF acts as a collecting house dealing with all matters that affect the policy and tactical doctrine used by the Infantry and the combined Arms of the Army. Within the SCHINF the Tactics Wing in particular assists in the formulation of Infantry policy regarding the development of possible future tactics, weapons, equipment and so forth. From this constant study also comes a continual assessment of the courses and course content provided by the School. By using the latest in education and training technology the SCHINF staff keep their training relevant, up-to-date and valid.

In practical terms, the SCHINF has on its books at any one time around 150 instructors, over 800 demonstration troops, approximately 300 training and administrative support personnel and some 500 civilians serving in various capacities. The numbers passing through the SCHINF vary from time to time but past years have seen an

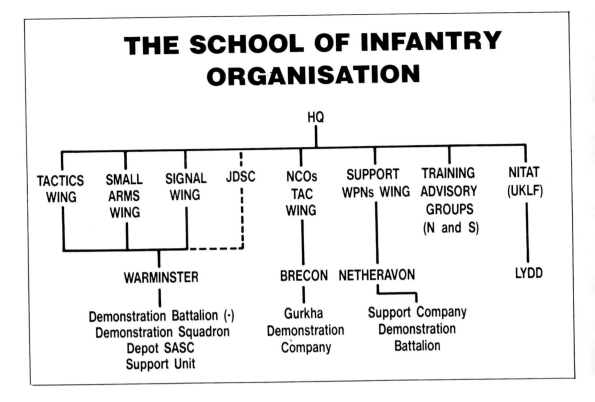

THE SCHOOL OF INFANTRY ORGANISATION

HQ

- TACTICS WING
- SMALL ARMS WING
- SIGNAL WING
- JDSC
- NCOs TAC WING
- SUPPORT WPNs WING
- TRAINING ADVISORY GROUPS (N and S)
- NITAT (UKLF)

WARMINSTER
- Demonstration Battalion (-)
- Demonstration Squadron
- Depot SASC
- Support Unit

BRECON
- Gurkha Demonstration Company

NETHERAVON
- Support Company Demonstration Battalion

LYDD

---

accumulation of well over 100,000 student days spent on courses every 12 months. Processing this number is no cheap exercise, for it has been calculated that each student day spent at the SCHINF costs approximately £500. That sum may seem high but it includes the cost of everything involved, from food and heating to the equipment and weapons.

SCHINF courses are provided for both officers and NCOs. To start with the best known courses it would be as well to consider what would happen to an Infantry officer leaving the Royal Military Academy at Sandhurst (RMAS). After successfully completing the full 44-week course at RMAS, most newly-commissioned officers join a regiment before attending a Platoon Commanders Battle Course (PCBC), held at the SCHINF. The PCBC is exactly what it says, a battle course for the newly-minted Infantry officer, who will be taught how to command his platoon in an All-Arms battle as well as in counter-revolutionary warfare. Four PCBCs are held each year.

The content of the PCBC has been determined following a thorough and painstaking examination of exactly what tasks a platoon commander has to carry out in battle. With the results of this study to hand it was then possible to draw up a list of training objectives to apply to the PCBC students. All the components of the PCBC can then be 'measured' to determine exactly how any student has fared. Using the same set of objectives, the training itself can be prepared and conducted to meet those objectives. In a way the PCBC can be used as an example of how the SCHINF staff use modern training technology to prepare and conduct the vast bulk of their training.

To return to the PCBC itself, there are usually 84 students in attendance, of which 12 places are for students from overseas. There are two main parts to the PCBC. The first part contains six weeks of skill-at-arms training covering all aspects of the required skills and knowledge for a platoon commander. This varies from the obvious skills in handling and firing all Infantry weapons to basic fieldcraft, minor tactics, first aid, map reading and land navigation and the all-important instructional techniques. Then follows the second part of the PCBC, eight weeks devoted to tactics where the student is put through the range of basic Infantry

Above:
A debrief after a tactical exercise using SAWES (Small Arms Weapons Effect Simulator).

Royal Engineers (RE), Royal Armoured Corps (RAC) and Royal Signals (R SIGNALS). The AATC is a highly practical course, for about 60% of the training time is spent out in the open undertaking all manner of exercises. As would be expected, the accent is on All-Arms co-operation. Later, as a Lieutenant-Colonel, an officer may return for the Commanding Officers Tactics Course (COTC) and possibly as a Brigadier for the Senior Officers Tactics Course (SOTC). Both courses are All-Arms courses.

The SCHINF runs many other officers' training courses, often in specialised subjects (such as Mortar Platoon Commander or Regimental Signal Officer), but the above-mentioned courses are among the most numerous carried out.

Other Ranks (OR) basic training is carried out using SCHINF guidelines. A recruit carries out his basic 14-week recruit training at his appropriate regimental depot and then progresses to further training within his battalion — all of which is carried out with the use of the SCHINF guidelines. The battalion is the fount of all OR training up to the point where the rank of Lance Corporal is attained and passed. Once the rank of Corporal has been attained it is time to attend the Section Commanders Battle Course, the SCBC.

The SCBC is a two-part course carried out by SCHINF instructors away from Warminster. The first part is a skill-at-arms course held at one of the SCHINF's two Training Advisory Groups (TAGs) at either Aldershot or Strensall; soldiers based in West Germany may attend a similar course held at Sennelager. The second part of the SCBC consists of six weeks of rigorous tactical training at the SCHINF's NCOs Tactical Wing at Brecon. Anyone getting through that six-week period will certainly know that they have been through a testing training course, but there is more to follow once the Corporal becomes a Sergeant. This time it is the Platoon Sergeants Battle Course (PSBC), an 11-week course again divided into two parts. The first part is carried out over four weeks at Warminster and mainly involves skill-at-arms. For the second part it is back to Brecon for a further seven weeks involving battle tactics. Once again the training is practical and carried out to the extent of using live firing wherever possible; operating under NBC conditions is heavily featured.

Further SCHINF training is provided for Staff Sergeants and WO2s but by then the training involved will be more specialised

tactics and operations, from pioneer techniques to ambushes and fighting in built-up areas (FIBUA).

The PCBC is again a practical one. Much of the time is spent out of the classroom undertaking practical exercises using troops from the Demonstration Battalion or fellow students. Live firing is carried out whenever possible and from time to time the Field Army outside the SCHINF is called upon to provide assistance with extra equipment and manpower such as AAC helicopters and their aircrews. This latter calling-in of outside support is common to many SCHINF courses.

Later in an Infantry officer's career a return to the SCHINF is certain. By the time the officer has reached the rank of Captain he will return for a All-Arms Tactics Course (AATC) where he will be one of 60 students from the Infantry, The Royal Artillery (RA),

Right:
A SAWES harness and projector. The harness carries several sensors that sense when a laser-based SAWES projector is being used against the wearer, ie the wearer is being 'fired' upon. If a sensor does receive a 'hit' the small box on the wearer's back starts to produce a loud sound that can only be switched off by the wearer lying on his back on top of the noise box. The SAWES projector can be seen on top of the L1A1 rifle. The system is being adapted for the SA80 weapon system.

and personal. Specialist courses are provided for personnel such as Sniper Instructors, Regimental Signallers and the support weapon commanders for Milan teams, mortars and the GPMG(SF). Many such specialised courses are carried out by the SCHINF or under SCHINF auspices, but at this point it would be as well to mention that all this training is not intended for the Regular Infantry alone. The SCHINF provides all the above-mentioned courses for the Territorial Army and Ulster Defence Regiment (UDR) as well, although (generally speaking) their courses tend to be shorter. From time to time the SCHINF also organises or carries out courses for students from countries that have purchased, or are purchasing, British defence equipments.

The above can provide only a very general outline of the activities of the SCHINF. In addition to the training outlined above, the SCHINF provides support for Defence Sales in the form of a small but highly versatile Sales Demonstration Team that travels to wherever it is needed. Fire-power and other demonstrations are laid on by the SCHINF

from time to time for the benefit of the various Staff Colleges and other interested parties. The various annual and other Inter-Service skill-at-arms meetings are usually organised and run by SCHINF personnel. At virtually any time, members of the SCHINF staff are away with the Field Army collecting views, information and generally keeping in touch with the end-product 'users'. More outside information comes to the School via international and inter-service cross-postings of selected personnel.

To add to all the above (which does not pretend to constitute a fully comprehensive list of SCHINF activities) the Commandant SCHINF commands the Warminster Garrison and is also responsible for the safety of much of the Salisbury Plain Training Area. This is no mean task in itself for on the Plain are numerous weapon ranges of all kinds and on any one day the SCHINF alone will be using some nine to 10 of them. More ranges are still being added, and by 1989 there will be an entirely new urban warfare training facility on the west end of the Plain.

8 The Small Arms School Corps

The Small Arms School Corps (SASC) has its origins in the Corps of Instructors which was formed in 1853. The crossed rifles and crown used in the SASC cap badge originate from that period — a period that will always associate the SASC with its long residence at Hythe in Kent. The move to Warminster was not made until 1969. The SASC as it is today was formed in 1929 and it has its head-quarters at Warminster where the Depot SASC is part of the Small Arms Wing of the School of Infantry (SCHINF); the Comman-dant SCHINF is also Commandant SASC.

The SASC is a small corps numbering only some 150 officers and men. It has an impact on the British Army far out of proportion to its numbers, an impact derived from what might be termed its Charter. Its primary role is 'To assist Regular and Territorial Army Infantry training units and battalions to achieve and maintain training standards for Small Arms and Support Weapons as decided by the Director of Infantry'. From those words stem the extremely high standards of proficiency in Infantry weapon skills that are the envy of many armed forces throughout the world. The words are emphasised by some of the secondary roles of the SASC. These roles include the advising of com-manders and staff on: (a) Small Arms and Support Weapons training, (b) Small Arms range courses and Support Weapons concen-trations (the get-togethers of as many support weapons personnel as possible, held on designated ranges ideally once every year), (c) range safety and the associated danger areas, and (not least in importance), (d) the development of Small Arms and Support Weapons. In addition to all the above the SASC assists the various Arms and Services (other than the Infantry) to achieve

the training standards laid down by the Arms/Services Directors for the handling of personal weapons and range safety.

To carry out all these functions the SASC is formed from volunteers from within the Army. The SASC attempt to recruit NCOs who are already experienced high-flyers, well into their Service careers and who have

Above:

A SASC officer demonstrating the preparation of the LAW 80.

SASC instructors using an 84mm L14A1 anti-tank gun. *MoD*

reached at least the rank of Corporal (although exceptionally Lance-Corporals are accepted). If they are accepted by the SASC they start as Sergeants and thereafter follow a career path within the SASC. Their introduction to the SASC is a Students Course during which the new man is taught how to teach, for teaching and instruction will thereafter be his primary function. If that course is successfully completed there follows a six-month probationary period during which the trainee carries out training under the supervision and guidance of other SASC instructors. At the end of that period the newly established member of the SASC can be posted to any of the locations where the SASC operates.

It must be stressed that all members of the SASC are already experienced soldiers when they volunteer for the SASC. Once in, they are trained to excel in training and advisory skills and are accordingly awarded high NCO rank. Usually, 20% of the SASC is made up of officers (who are commissioned from within the SASC), 10% are WO1s and the rest are WO2s, Staff Sergeants or Sergeants. They may find themselves posted to a number of locations. Some are posted to the School of Infantry (SCHINF) at Warminster or its Support Weapons Wing at Netheravon. Others are located within the two Training Advisory Groups (TAGs) at Aldershot and Catterick while some may be posted to the Infantry Trials and Development Unit (ITDU) at Warminster. More SASC personnel will be found at Infantry Depots and the various Divisions, Commands and headquarters throughout the Army and at training establishments such as the Royal Military Academy at Sandhurst (RMAS).

Wherever they are to be found, SASC personnel will be busy carrying out or administering training. In both their training and advisory capacities the SASC has quite an influence on the fire conduct of the Army. The Army is not strong in numbers or the degree of fire-power it can place in the field, so every shot fired has to be to good effect. This means a high standard of weapon handling, individual weapon accuracy and fire control, all coupled to a demand for firearms safety at all times, ie skill-at-arms. In all of these fields the SASC makes its mark. SASC instructors have for many years been renowned for their all-round skill-at-arms and SASC personnel always seem to feature in the winners' lists of the various inter-Service and other rifle meets held at Bisley and elsewhere. These manifestations of ability are backed up by the imparting of these skills by the teaching and training methods used by the SASC.

The advent of the automatic fire personal weapon has brought with it a dramatic increase in ammunition consumption within many armed forces, mainly by the unchecked application of the 'Beirut Syndrome'. This has not happened within the British Army for the simple reason that the training carried out by the SASC continually emphasises the need for strict fire control at all times. All Army personnel are trained in the need for deliberate aim at designated targets and for the conservation of ammunition. This strict fire control discipline can soon be lost, as many armed forces have already discovered to their cost, but the SASC in its quiet but efficient way ensures that, via their training and advice, matters are kept under control. One offshoot of this strict fire control is a reduction in the overall logistic burden for the Army. Reduced small arms ammunition expenditure means a reduced resupply load for support troops to handle, leaving more logistic capacity for other essential items.

The SASC is involved in the testing and development of new weapons and equipment at the Infantry Trials and Development Unit (ITDU), based at Warminster. Any new weapon that enters service does so only after it has been extensively trialled and tested under the supervision of the ITDU and at the same time training requirements and methods are investigated and laid down for the eventual introduction into service. In recent years several new weapons have entered service and the SASC in the ITDU have been heavily involved. At present the 30mm Rarden Gun is one of the SASC's biggest training projects, along with LAW 80 and others. These new weapons often involve the introduction of new training methods, for the SASC is constantly updating its training techniques and keeping abreast of training developments wherever they occur. At present, simulators of all kinds are under development (or are already in service) and more use of them can be expected in the future.

The SASC also has an international flavour. It provides instructors and advisors for the Sultan of Oman's armed forces and at any one time exchange postings are being carried out with similar establishments in Australia and Canada. Exchange postings are also carried out between the SASC and the Royal Marines.

Below:
A SASC instructor demonstrating the L42A1 sniper rifle from a non-tactical position.

9 Preparing for Warrior

One of the largest training tasks the Infantry has in prospect at the time of writing is the programme involved in getting the Warrior infantry combat vehicle into service. It is such a large programme with so many long-term ramifications that no account of the modern Infantry would be complete without detailed consideration of the Warrior conversion programme.

Perhaps the first thing to consider regarding the Warrior training package is the question of why it is necessary at all. That can be readily answered by saying that for the Infantry, Warrior is something entirely new. Warrior is not just a new type of vehicle but a totally new weapon system of a kind the Infantry have never had to deal with before. Warrior involves, among other things, a crew-served turret, a powerful new gun with all the associated fire control and other drills,

plus the tactics involved with such an armoured platform. Past experience with the Scimitar reconnaissance vehicles cannot really be applied to Warrior. The number of personnel involved with Scimitar within a battalion is relatively small and their training has been carried out by the Royal Armoured Corps (RAC) for some years.

Thus the Infantry have virtually no experience of the handling of similar armoured vehicles to fall back upon. The FV432 is no real guide to handling Warrior as it is simply not a true fighting vehicle, being nothing more than a rather basic and simple armoured personnel carrier with only limited armament and devoid of anything like a crew-served turret (apart from the small number of Rarden-armed FV432s used in Berlin, and they can be disregarded in training and experience terms).

Right:
An early Warrior prototype photographed during a demonstration held in Germany.

Far right:
A Warrior on the ranges.

Faced with the prospect of a major training programme, Infantry staff planners decided to undertake a radical step at an early stage. They assembled several commercial industrial training concerns and placed their training requirements before them. They were then asked to come up with a solution. Eventually a consortium of companies, headed by Alvis Ltd and including Invertron and Rediffusion, was selected and their solution is, at the time of writing, in the final stages of development to be ready to initiate the Warrior conversion training programme. The first conversion course was scheduled to be carried out at Munster between January and March 1988. That course involved the 1st Battalion Grenadier Guards (1 GREN GDS), the first operational unit to be issued with Warrior. They will be followed by the 1st Battalion, The Staffordshire Regiment (1 STAFFORDS) during the autumn of 1988.

By the time the conversion programme has been completed in spring 1994, there will be 13 Armoured Infantry battalions equipped with Warrior. Each battalion will have 45 Warriors and, for each vehicle, training will have to be provided for the driver, commander, deputy commander and gunner. Training the driver is relatively straightforward but the other crew members have to undergo a more involved course.

The Warrior conversion course lasts 12 weeks with a further two weeks devoted to live firing on the Soltau ranges. The fairly intensive course is conducted at the battalion's location in West Germany and is carried out under the guidance of the Armoured Infantry Training and Advisory Team (AITAT) who will be based at Sennelager and travel to wherever the current training location happens to be at any one time. The AITAT supervises the conversion training and provides guidance (and instructors if needed), but the actual training is carried out by an instruction team from within the battalion involved. The battalion gunnery instructors are trained at Lulworth and the driving and maintenance instructors at Bovington. When they return to their battalions actually to carry out the conversion programme, they have available a selection of the training aids and simulators provided by the industry team mentioned previously.

The conversion course is fairly intense and makes use of a number of simulators. The simplest of these is a classroom weapon stand that is little more than an open stand carrying a 30mm Rarden Gun and a 7.62mm L94A1 Chain Gun mounted side-by-side exactly as they would be in a Warrior turret. It is used to familiarise the Warrior crew students with their main weapons and, as the students are seated behind the guns in exactly the same position as in a Warrior turret, the stand is used for hands-on

55

training involving loading and unloading drills, clearing jams and simple in-turret maintenance.

The next stage in gunnery training involves the use of a computer based Desk Top Trainer. As its name implies, this device is located on a classroom desk and consists of a sight visor and the associated gunnery controls, plus a simple computer used by an instructor to control the system. As a student looks into the visor, he sees the weapon sight graticule imposed upon a screen on to which a simulated landscape and targets can be introduced. The student then uses the sights and the gun controls to acquire and engage the targets with the appropriate weapon (ie Rarden or Chain Gun). For this trainer the imagery is simple but it provides adequate simulation for the gunnery student learning the basics of target acquisition and engagement. The progress and results of an engagement are presented to an instructor on a monitor screen and can be recorded to provide play-backs and act as the source of further instruction. As an alternative, the Desk Top Trainer can be 'driven' by the student at his own pace and can be used for refresher as well as basic training, as will be outlined later.

The Turret Trainer is a step up from the Desk Top Trainer. This involves training for both the gunner and commander who are located in a simulator that closely resembles the interior of a Warrior turret. The turret interior contains all the usual controls in exactly the right locations and the realism is even carried to the point of using a real co-axial L94A1 Chain Gun — the Rarden is a realistic dummy. Within the Turret Trainer the crew are provided with weapon sights and vision devices into which simulated landscapes and targets are introduced to provide training in acquiring and engaging targets with the crew working together. The trainer can be used to simulate day or night vision conditions. Also simulated are firing sounds and projectile tracer paths; hits are graphically indicated. Once again the simu-

Below:
The interior of Warrior showing the turret bustle surrounded by a wire mesh screen.

lated imagery is basic and the results are presented to an instructor on a monitor screen. The monitor is mounted on a fixture over the trainer so that other students can witness and learn from the training in progress. Once the basics of working together have been absorbed by the student turret crew, the Turret Trainer can be used for a series of firing exercises using pre-prepared training sequences inserted into the computer-controlled system on floppy discs.

There is one further Warrior simulator and that is the Platoon Trainer. The first of these was scheduled to be ready during August 1988 and basically consists of four Turret Trainers linked together to enable a platoon of Warrior turret crews to train as a team. The four Turret Trainers are located with each in its own mobile ISO container and are linked via a central computer. This computer not only controls and monitors the system but produces computer-generated imagery that is far more realistic and involved than the simple images used on the Desk Top and basic Turret Trainers. The computer produces the overall terrain 'model' (a real piece of ground in Germany) in which the Warrior

platoon operates and each of the four student crews have their own individual outlook on to that model. In practical terms this means that one crew could see a target that is invisible to another, just as during real engagements, so platoon fire control can be realistically carried out by the Platoon Commander. For training, the system can produce up to 20 targets of which up to 12 targets (six static and six moving) can be presented at any one time. The degree of image realism is such that accurate recognition of various types of target is possible. As a bonus the Platoon Trainer can be used as four individual Turret Trainers with the added attraction of involving the more realistic computer-synthesised imagery. Again, the Platoon Trainer can simulate a variety of terrain and vision conditions and can be used to carry out prolonged exercises, some lasting hours if required. Only four Platoon Trainers will be produced and two of

Below:
Interior view of a command Warrior showing folded map tables and working surfaces.

Above:
The end product — Infantry debussing from a Warrior. *1 (BR) Corps*

them will travel around to be used for refresher training within already-converted battalions as well as for the conversion courses; the other two will be based at static locations in Sennelager and Hohne.

Not all the training is on simulators for the Warrior course also involves a considerable amount of conventional classroom training employing the usual array of wall charts, videos, tape/slide lessons, view-foils, manuals and flip charts. Some of the maintenance training involves models and cross-sectioned vehicle and engine components and there is plenty of practical work.

Once the conversion course has been completed, the various simulators and training aids used on the course (apart from the Platoon Trainer) are retained by the battalion to be used for in-house refresher training. This is particularly important as far as gunnery is concerned for within most battalions live firing will usually be restricted to one range session per year.

It is planned that two battalions will convert to the Armoured Infantry role each year. Once the conversion is complete the battalion will accumulate experience and expertise that cannot be allowed to be dissipated once the battalion ends its tour. To this end, as each tour is completed a team of experienced personnel in specific appointments within the battalion will remain on station to carry over their experience and knowedge to the next battalion converting to Warrior. This carry-over increment will be known as the Armoured Infantry Manning Increment (AIMI) and will consist of a team of 72 personnel having a cross-section of the various Warrior skill and experience requirements. Some of them will remain with the new battalion for a period of six months or so, while others will remain for up to 18 months before rejoining (hopefully) their original battalion. It is anticipated that these increments will be produced from within the various Infantry Divisions. The first of these AIMI exercises will not be carried out until some time during early 1991 when the first Armoured Infantry battalion moves out of role.

10 Infantry in the Territorial Army

Over the last few decades the Territorial Army (TA) has undergone a radical change. It used to be a source of volunteer soldiers who could be called upon to help out the Regulars only in an emergency and it was trained, equipped and treated accordingly. Those strictures no longer apply. Today the TA is an integral part of the British Army to the extent that the Regulars could not carry out their commitments without the active involvement of the part-time volunteers who form the bulk of the TA. The TA now acts as an immediate reinforcement force for the British commitment to NATO and also forms the bulk of the Home Defence force in an emergency.

An indication of the importance of the TA to today's Army can be seen by the number of TA Infantry battalions. By 1 April 1990, when the current process of raising new battalions will be complete, there will be 41 TA Infantry battalions — three of them from the Parachute Regiment. Of this total, 14 battalions are allotted to Home Defence while the other 27 have a NATO role.

The 38 TA Infantry battalions (plus the three PARA battalions) are the result of a recent reorganisation of the TA which will be completed by April 1990. The reorganisation has been carried out in two phases, the most recent of which included the raising of six new TA Infantry battalions. The reorganisation will eventually have achieved two ends. One is to make the internal structure of the TA much easier to administer, both geographically and logistically. The previous TA organisation meant that within some battalions companies or other units were often scattered all around the United Kingdom in such a way that even routine administration was made unduly difficult. The new battalions are distributed into much-reduced geographical areas, and at the same time the opportunity has been made to ensure that the TA battalions are much closer in establishment strengths to their Regular counterparts.

While the establishment strengths of the TA battalions might be similar to those of the Regulars, their internal organisations differ. Most TA battalions now have four Rifle Companies (one even has five) but they do not have a separate Fire Support Company. Instead the Headquarters Company contains the support weapons. In the case of a NATO-roled battalion there are six Milan Firing Posts and six 81mm mortars (battalions assigned to the 2nd Infantry Division have eight 81mm mortars). Each Company will, in due course, have three GPMG(SF)s; at the time of writing each platoon had three GPMGs. Home Defence battalions have no Milans and (at the time of writing) only two 81mm mortars.

All TA Infantry battalions travel on wheels using, in the main, 4-tonne trucks or Land Rovers. Plans to equip some NATO-roled TA battalions with the Saxon wheeled armoured personnel carrier have so far come to nothing and it seems unlikely that any Saxons will be procured for the TA during the foreseeable future. Even the reconnaissance sections of a TA battalion rely on Land Rovers. In an emergency it is expected that any shortfalls in transport will be made up with requisitioned vehicles, especially in the case of the Home Defence battalions who are lightly equipped overall.

From the above it will be seen that, although the TA forms an immediate reinforcement force for the Regular Army, it is relatively less well equipped, especially in

Above:
A Warrior at Warminster.

combat transport. There are plans that the bulk of the TA Infantry will be equipped with SA80 by 1992 and with the new weapons will gradually come the latest improvements in uniforms and other equipment. The intention to equip the TA on a par with the Regulars is always there but the costs involved are high.

At present there are plenty of volunteers for the TA Infantry battalions to the extent that establishment levels usually run at almost 100%, although as always with such voluntary organisations there is a constant turnover of personnel. Historically this turnover runs at about 30% of total, a figure matched by similar organisations elsewhere. However, the population of most battalions is not necessarily all effectives. At any one time the head count includes recruits under training. Set against this every battalion has its central core of long-term volunteers and

in an emergency the volunteers would be joined by reservists and reserve officers.

Training for TA volunteers is almost all carried out within the local unit. From time to time some specialised courses are undertaken at Regular establishments (usually the local Divisional or Regimental Depot, although some courses are carried out by or at the School of Infantry — qv) but the greater part of the training is carried out in drill halls during weekday evenings and at weekends. Weekend training may be carried out at nearby training areas and often involves overnight exercises. Every couple of years or so full scale national exercises are undertaken and the NATO-roled battalions may find themselves carrying out their annual 15-day training period in West Germany. Volunteers are supposed to undertake to attend a number of weekday or weekend training parades every year in addition to the annual 15-day training. Many individuals exceed these commitments by a considerable degree, no doubt attracted by the high level of varied social activity that takes place within the TA outside its purely military existence, although this alone is not

the full reason — many attend simply because they are keen.

Most TA Infantry battalions are commanded by a Regular officer and other key posts are manned by Regular officers and Senior NCOs. Every battalion has a Regular Training Major and the Battalion Adjutant usually falls into the same category. The Regimental Sergeant Major is also a Regular. Each Rifle Company has a Regular Senior NCO Permanent Staff Instructor (PSI), in NATO-roled battalions a WO2 known as the Senior Permanent Staff Instructor. NATO-roled battalions also have a Regular Staff Sergeant for each Rifle Company.

The routine administration load in a TA battalion is considerable so each battalion has a small civilian staff to assist, usually including an ex-Regular Permanent Staff Administration Officer (PSAO) — NATO-roled battalions also have a Regular Quartermaster.

The TA Infantry battalions are now an integral part of the overall Infantry strength of the British Army. The fact that the vast bulk of TA personnel are part-time soldiers does not mean that they have part-time

Above:
A Corporal from a Queen's Regiment TA battalion demonstrating the firing of the L1A1 SLR when fitted with the 30-round magazine from the L4A4 light machine gun.

standards. Their personal dedication to their duties and the spirit with which they train should leave no-one in any doubt that they are just as much a part of the British Infantry as any Regular.

The TA Infantry battalions are listed below.

The Scottish Division

1st Battalion, 52nd Lowland Volunteers (1/52 LOWLAND)
2nd Battalion, 52nd Lowland Volunteers (2/52 LOWLAND)
1st Battalion, 51st Highland Volunteers (1/51 HIGHLAND)
2nd Battalion, 51st Highland Volunteers (2/51 HIGHLAND)
3rd Battalion, 51st Highland Volunteers (3/51 HIGHLAND)

The Queen's Division

5th (Volunteer) Battalion The Queen's Regiment (5 QUEENS)
6th/7th (Volunteer) Battalion The Queen's Regiment (6/7 QUEENS)
8th (Volunteer) Battalion The Queen's Fusiliers (City of London) (8 QF)
5th (Volunteer) Battalion The Royal Regiment of Fusiliers (5 RRF)
6th (Volunteer) Battalion The Royal Regiment of Fusiliers (6 RRF)
5th (Volunteer) Battalion The Royal Anglian Regiment (5 R ANGLIAN)
6th (Volunteer) Battalion The Royal Anglian Regiment (6 R ANGLIAN)
7th (Volunteer).Battalion The Royal Anglian Regiment (7 R ANGLIAN)

The King's Division

4th (Volunteer) Battalion The King's Own Royal Border Regiment (4 KINGS OWN BORDER)

Below:
TA soldier demonstrating the Mk 3 NBC 'Noddy' suit.

5th/8th (Volunteer) Battalion The King's Regiment (5/8 KINGS)
4th (Volunteer) Battalion The Queen's Lancashire Regiment (4 QLR)
1st Battalion The Yorkshire Volunteers (1 YORKS)
2nd Battalion The Yorkshire Volunteers (2 YORKS)
3rd Battalion The Yorkshire Volunteers (3 YORKS)
4th Battalion The Yorkshire and Cleveland Volunteers (4 YORKS)
4th (Volunteer) Battalion The Royal Irish Rangers (The North Irish Militia) (4 R IRISH)
5th (Volunteer) Battalion The Royal Irish Rangers (5 R IRISH)

The Prince of Wales' Division

4th (Volunteer) Battalion The Devonshire and Dorset Regiment (4 D and D)
3rd (Volunteer) Battalion The Cheshire Regiment (3 CHESHIRE)
1st Battalion The Wessex Regiment (Rifle Volunteers) (1 WESSEX)
2nd Battalion the Wessex Regiment (Volunteers) (2 WESSEX)
3rd Battalion The Staffordshire Regiment (Prince of Wales' Own) (3 STAFFORDS)
3rd (Volunteer) Battalion The Royal Welch Fusiliers (3 RWF)
3rd (Volunteer) Battalion The Royal Regiment of Wales (3 RRW)
4th (Volunteer) Battalion The Royal Regiment of Wales (4 RRW)
3rd (Volunteer) Battalion The Worcestershire and Sherwood Foresters Regiment (3 WFR)
4th (Volunteer) Battalion The Worcestershire and Sherwood Foresters Regiment (4 WFR)

The Light Division

5th Battalion The Light Infantry (Volunteers) (5 LI)
6th Battalion The Light Infantry (Volunteers) (6 LI)
7th Battalion The Light Infantry (Volunteers) (7 LI)
8th Battalion The Light Infantry (Volunteers) (8 LI)
4th (Volunteer) Battalion The Royal Green Jackets (4 RGJ)
5th (Volunteer) Battalion The Royal Green Jackets (5 RGJ)

11 Combat Vehicles

FV510 Warrior

Crew:	3+7
Combat weight:	24,500kg
Length:	6.34m
Width:	3.034m
Height, overall:	2.735m
Height to hull roof:	1.93m
Ground clearance:	490mm
Track width:	460mm
Max road speed:	75km/hr
Road range:	500km
Fuel capacity:	772 litres
Gradient:	60%
Fording:	1.3m
Engine:	Rolls-Royce CV8 TCA V-8 diesel developing 550hp at 2,300rpm
Armament:	1×30mm L21A1 Rarden gun 1×7.62mm L94A1 Chain Gun

The FV510 Warrior is the main armoured personnel carrier used by the Armoured Infantry battalions and was previously known as MCV-80. At one time it was intended that Warrior/MCV-80 would replace the FV432 but, for the foreseeable future, Warrior will only supplement the FV432.

Warrior had its design origins as long ago as 1967, but it was 1971 before paper feasibility studies were completed. After those it was 1978 before project definitions were ready and even then there was a parallel evaluation between the then MCV-80 and the American XM2 (now the M2 'Bradley'). With the selection of MCV-80, GKN Defence Operations were given the go-ahead to commence detailed design work in 1979.

It was 1980 before the first prototypes were running. Then followed a period of trials and all manner of testing before full production was ordered in 1985. Production is now well under way at Telford in Shropshire and the first vehicle was handed over to the Army in mid-1987.

The Warrior has an all-aluminium hull that not only reduces overall weight but provides better protection for the occupants and crew than that afforded by the FV432; the armour is proof against 155mm artillery projectile fragments and 14.5mm machine gun fire. The layout of the standard FV150 Warrior platoon vehicle is such that the driver sits forward on the left and next to the powerpack compartment. The commander, who is also the section commander, sits in the two-man turret along with the gunner for the 30mm Rarden gun that forms the vehicle's main armament together with a co-axial 7.62mm L94A1 Chain Gun. Night vision devices are provided. A door in the hull rear provides access and egress for the remaining seven members of the section. They are seated along bench seats, four on the right and three on the left but there is no provision for them to use their weapons from within the hull. Roof hatches are fitted; in action these would remain closed. There is space under the seats and in internal racks for kit plus more space in stowage boxes located on either side of the main door, and the Warrior can carry enough stores to maintain an Infantry section in action for 48hr without replenishment (apart from fuel). The interior is fully NBC sealed and there is a full NBC ventilation system.

For the travelling soldiers the main item of note regarding Warrior is its smooth ride. The torsion bar suspension irons out the worst of the usual jolts and bumps suffered by the occupants of most similar vehicles, so

Facing page:
A Warrior showing its paces through North German mud. *1 (BR) Corps*

Inset:
Prior to receiving its current designation, the FV510 Warrior was known as *MCV-80*. One of the prototypes is shown here undergoing field trials before the commencement of production in 1985. *Army Public Information UKLF*

Above:
A rear view of one of the MCV-80 prototypes. The two-piece rear door was replaced by a single one on the production vehicle.
Army Public Information UKLF

when the time comes to debus the soldiers are not so tired and knocked about as they might otherwise be. Driving the Warrior is also much easier than driving the FV432 and many other similar vehicles — the basics can be mastered in a very short time as the author can testify.

A new aspect of Infantry combat introduced by Warrior will be the tactical use of the vehicles once their occupants have disembarked. If the commander dismounts that will leave the vehicle manned only by the driver and gunner. During most combat situations the section commander will remain in the vehicle, for, although it is possible for the gunner to load and fire the main gun by himself, the full potential of the turret cannot be fully realised without his

presence. All the time radios will have to be operated, routine orders taken and various other operations carried out. The potential firepower of Warrior is too precious to leave out of combat once the section has departed. The argument as to how that potential firepower could be deployed to support the section or platoon has not yet been fully resolved. There is no place on the battlefield for the Warrior to be used as a general anti-armour vehicle, for the 30mm Rarden cannot tackle battle tanks and the armour is not proof against most anti-armour weapons. The general thinking is that the manpower of a Warrior platoon will have to be regarded as three dismounted fire sections with a further section manning the empty vehicles. The platoon vehicles can then be used to provide fire support from the flanks or where they can be best employed either in attack or in defence. There are also plans to use Warriors as screening vehicles on the flanks or in front of fixed positions.

The bulk of Warrior production will be the basic FV510 platoon vehicle described above. Another variant to be used by the Infantry will be the Warrior command vehicle which will retain the turret and armament of the platoon vehicle but with the interior configured for the command role with extra lighting, radios, map tables and other equipment. Operating with the Infantry will be the Warrior armoured repair and recovery vehicles (ARRVs — seven to every Armoured Infantry battalion) of the Royal Electrical and

Mechanical Engineers (REME). These ARRVs will have a small turret armed only with a 7.62mm L94A1 Chain Gun and they will also be recognisable by the hydraulic crane jib carried along the hull roof on the left-hand side. Internally the ARRVs will be provided with tools, spares and equipment to keep the other vehicles of the Armoured Infantry battalions moving.

The only other Warrior variants likely to be seen in the near future will be Royal Artillery mechanised artillery observation vehicles (MAOV) that will also operate alongside the Armoured Infantry. In armament and outward appearance this variant will be identical to the Warrior platoon vehicle, but it will be fitted with a wide variety of radios, observation and survey equipment to provide target data for the Artillery batteries. There will be so much of this special equipment that the turret will have to mount a dummy gun. There will also be Artillery battery command vehicles (BAV) belonging to battery commanders providing direct support for the Battle Groups.

More Warrior variants are not anticipated in the immediate future, despite early plans to provide mortar carriers and perhaps some other types. The main reason for this has been that the Warrior has proved to be a rather expensive vehicle — so expensive in fact that the numbers produced will be limited to 1,053. The FV432s will have to be retained in service, even within the Armoured Infantry battalions where they will continue to be used by the Headquarters and Fire Support Companies.

FV432

Crew:	2+10
Combat weight:	15,280kg
Length:	5.251m
Width:	2.8m
Height to hull top:	1.879m
Ground clearance:	406mm
Track width:	343mm
Max road speed:	52.2km/hr
Road range:	480km
Fuel capacity:	454 litres
Fording:	1.066m
Gradient:	60%
Engine:	Rolls-Royce K60 No 4 Mk 4F developing 240bhp at 3,750rpm
Armament:	see text

Over the years the FV432 armoured personnel carrier (APC) has been the backbone of the Mechanised Infantry battalions of 1 (BR) Corps and is set to remain the main carrier for the Mechanised (Tracked) Infantry battalions for the immediate future.

The FV432 is a product of the early 1960s and was a development of the earlier FV420 series of vehicles. It was 1961 when the FV432 prototype appeared and production

Far left:
A 'flat top' FV432 with a 7.62mm L7A2 machine gun mounted on the commander's cupola.

Left:
The FV432 interior.

followed soon after, ending in 1971. Early examples (Mk 1) were fitted with petrol engines but later variants (Mk 2) used diesels and today any remaining petrol-engined variants are used for training only. Production was carried out by GKN Sankey, now GKN Defence Operations.

In design terms the FV432 is a self-propelled armoured box on tracks. Steel is used for the hull with the driver seated to the right next to the powerpack compartment. The vehicle commander is provided with a roof-mounted cupola located just behind the driver and most of the rest of the roof area is taken up by a circular hatch and its covers. The Infantry section enters and leaves the vehicle via a large door in the hull rear. Inside the hull, bench seating is provided along each side wall with the occupants facing inwards; there is no provision for occupants other than the commander to use their weapons from within the hull (other than through the roof hatch) and there are no vision devices for them to observe the outside world once the vehicle is closed down. This lack of outside reference can give rise to a brief but awkward period of disorientation as the occupants leave the vehicle.

FV432s are provided with an NBC system but otherwise the standard vehicle is very simple. The basic form of the FV432 can be used to provide a whole family of variants, only a few of which are used by the Infantry. The FV432 family includes repair vehicles, specialised Artillery vehicles (including the FV433 Abbot 105mm self-propelled gun), signal and command vehicles.

Infantry FV432 variants start with the various forms of armament. The basic armament of the FV432 is a single 7.62mm L7A2 GPMG mounted on a pintle by the commander's hatch. While such an arrangement is effective it provides no cover for the commander when firing the weapon, so many 1 (BR) Corps FV432s use a small traversing turret to protect the commander and machine gun, in this case the 7.62mm L37A1. The turret is located on the hull roof in place of the usual roof hatch. A small hatch to the rear of the turret allows the commander to raise his head for observation when it is safe to do so and smoke dischargers are located along each side of the turret. The turret can traverse through 360° and the machine gun can be elevated 50° to provide some measure of defence against low-flying aircraft, or helicopters. Aiming the L37A1 machine gun is assisted by the insertion of extra tracer rounds into the ammunition belts to make fire trajectories more visible through the gun's reflex sight. The usual ratio of L37A1 turret-armed FV432s to pintle-armed FV432s is usually 2:2 but in some battalions it may be 3:1.

At one stage of the FV432's service career, the turret concept was taken one step further with the adoption of a gun turret very similar to that used by the FV721 Fox which mounted a 30mm L21A1 Rarden gun. A batch of 13 FV432s were converted to this

configuration and for a while were used for troop trials but they were not adopted generally. The reasons for this appear to have been several. One must have been that the bulky turret made the FV432/turret combination rather top-heavy and unwieldy while the turret bustle occupied most of the available space within the hull, leaving little room for other personnel or anything else. Accordingly the converted vehicles were assigned to the Berlin Brigade where they remain.

In the tracked Fire Support Company the FV432 is used to carry the dismounted Milan teams. Each FV432 carries two Milan FPs and their two-man teams with Milan launchers and missile containers carried internally on special racks.

Also in the tracked Fire Support Company are FV432s converted to carry the L16A1 81mm mortar. Each of these FV432 variants carries a single mortar firing through the roof hatch from a mounting on a floor-mounted turntable with a full 360° traverse. Internal racks are fitted to carry up to 160 bombs. Weight in action of a mortar FV432 is about 16,400kg and the crew is four to six men.

Above:
FV432s with L37 turrets are paraded by soldiers of the Royal Irish Rangers.

Right:
One of the few FV432s fitted with a turret mounting a 30mm Rarden Gun.

Far right:
The wheeled Saxon armoured personnel carrier.

Ambulance FV432s can operate with the Infantry. They are unarmed and can carry up to four stretchers, two on each side. If two stretchers are not fitted there is also seating for up to five walking casualties.

The only other Infantry FV432 is a command vehicle. This is a basic vehicle equipped for the command role carrying extra radios and items such as map tables and wall boards. A feature of these command vehicles is the canvas 'penthouse' extension that can be erected over the rear door to provide cover for the constant stream of visitors to command vehicles. The penthouse can also be used to join up with other command vehicles to form a larger command post centre. When folded down the penthouse is carried on the vehicle hull or sides. The command FV432 usually has a crew of seven.

Although it is not very often so used, the basic FV432 can be used as an armoured cargo carrier once the internal seating has been removed or folded away. Each vehicle can then carry up to 3,670kg of ammunition or other stores.

The FV432 is now set for a service life that will extend into the 21st century. By then most of them will be well over 30 years old and many will no doubt be feeling their age. Most are already well used and in need of careful maintenance and constant attention so one can only wonder how many will fare after a further extension to their military careers.

Consideration is being given to the replacement for the FV432. Cost consider- ations seem to preclude any future large-scale procurement of more Warriors so a lighter and less costly vehicle now known only as the Future Light 'A' Vehicle is currently in the concept definition stage. It will be only one vehicle in a projected range of vehicles known as the Future Families of Light Armoured Vehicles (FFLAV) that will replace many light armoured vehicles now used by the Army. Whatever form the Future Light 'A' Vehicle might take, it is a long way from any introduction into service.

AT105 Saxon

Crew:	2 + 8
Weight in action:	11,660kg
Length:	5.169m
Width:	2.489m
Height, commander's cupola:	2.628m
Ground clearance, axles:	290mm
Wheelbase:	3.073m
Track, front/rear:	2.08m/1.99m
Max road speed:	96km/hr
Road range:	480km
Fuel capacity:	153 litres
Gradient:	60%
Fording:	1.12m
Engine:	Bedford 500 6-cylinder diesel developing 164bhp at 2,800rpm
Armament:	1 × 7.62mm L7A2 machine gun

A command Saxon with penthouse extension erected. *GKN Defence Operations*

The Saxon wheeled 4 × 4 armoured personnel carrier is the main 'battle waggon' of the Mechanised (Wheeled) Infantry Battalions and is thus used by Infantry units based in the United Kingdom who have to travel to Germany in an emergency to take up their battle stations. The main users are 19 Infantry Brigade who are headquartered at Colchester. In time of war they will form part of the 3rd Armoured Division and thus have a lengthy journey in prospect. Such a journey can be made far more comfortably and rapidly on wheels rather than on tracks, so hence the introduction of Saxon.

Saxon had its origins in an internal security vehicle known as the AT104 produced by GKN Sankey, now GKN Defence Operations. The AT104 evolved into the dual purpose AT105 armoured personnel carrier/ internal security vehicle which was originally developed as an export venture but which attracted the attention of the British Army in view of its realignment of some combat formations from BAOR to the United Kingdom. During early 1983 the Army placed orders for 47 AT105s, by then known as the

Saxon, and an order for a further 200 was placed in 1985. Production was still under way at the time of writing.

Saxons used by the Infantry differ in several aspects from the original AT105s. The most obvious modification is the addition of stowage boxes to several parts of the hull exterior, and these will be very necessary once the Saxons start their journey as they will virtually be homes for their occupants for extended periods of time. More stowage space is provided in a rudimentary roof rack. Welded steel plate is used for the hull and the vehicle chassis and the drive train is based on commercial components — many taken from the Bedford MK truck. At the front the driver sits on the right next to the engine compartment which is protected by flame-proof ventilation louvres. The driver's vision ports are bulletproof, as are all vision ports on the Saxon. Run-flat tyres are fitted as standard. Access to the vehicle is via a double door at the hull rear; the driver and commander have their own roof hatches. On the roof the commander is provided with a fixed cupola with a DISA mounting for a 7.62mm L7A2 GPMG. Smoke dischargers are also fitted. Inside the hull the passengers are seated on padded bench seats and seat belts are provided.

Each Mechanised (Wheeled) Infantry Battalion has 43 Saxons. Some of these are

command vehicles fitted with the usual command post paraphernalia and each battalion also has a REME recovery Saxon with a side-mounted 5,000kg recovery winch. It is possible that an ambulance variant will emerge one day — a prototype has already been trialled. There are long-term plans to provide extra Saxons to carry Milan teams.

At one time there were hopes that sufficient Saxons would be procured to provide armoured personnel carriers for at least some Territorial Army Infantry units who would have to travel to West Germany in an emergency. To date these hopes have remained unfulfilled.

FV103 Spartan
(Data for MCT version in brackets where different)

Crew:	3+4 [3]
Weight in action:	8,172 [8,342]kg
Length:	4.93m
Width:	2.257m
Height:	2.28 [3.38]m
Ground clearance:	356mm
Track width:	432mm
Max road speed:	80.5km/hr
Road range:	483km
Fuel capacity:	386 [350] litres
Gradient:	60%

Above:
A FV103 Spartan CVR(T) fitted with twin Milan launchers on the Milan Compact Turret.

Fording:	1.067m
Engine:	Jaguar J60 No 1 Mk 100B petrol developing 190bhp at 4,750rpm
Armament:	1×7.62mm L7A2 machine gun [MCT 2×Milan ready to fire]

The FV103 Spartan is part of the CVR(T) range based on the Scorpion and Scimitar reconnaissance vehicles. It is the armoured personnel carrier component of the range and as such was never intended to be a replacement for the FV432 series; its internal capacity is only seven men, including the crew. Instead the Spartan was developed as a special purpose carrier that can be used by any number of specialist teams. With the Infantry the Spartan has two roles.

Within the tracked mechanised battalions the Spartan is used as the carrier for the Mortar Fire Controllers (MFC). Four vehicles are used for this purpose while elsewhere in the Fire Support Company the Spartan is used by the Mobile Section of the Anti-tank

Platoon where it is fitted with a roof-mounted Milan Compact Turret (MCT). In armoured and mechanised (tracked) battalions, four Spartans with three-man crews carry out the mobile medium range anti-tank role. One man is the driver, another acts as the vehicle commander and missile tracker from a station in the turret while the third man handles the missile containers and assists in reloading the twin-missile launcher. The MCT can carry two Milans ready to fire and there is space internally for a further eight missiles.

FV105 Sultan

Crew:	5 or 6
Combat weight:	8,664kg
Length:	4.8m
Width:	2.254m
Height overall:	2.559m
Ground clearance:	0.356m
Track width:	432mm
Max road speed:	72.5km/hr
Road range:	483km
Gradient:	60%

Above:
A MCT Spartan at speed on the Sennelager ranges.

Right:
A Sultan command vehicle.

Fording:	1.067m
Engine:	Jaguar J60 No 1 Mk 100B petrol developing 190bhp at 4,750rpm
Armament	1×7.62mm L7A2 machine gun

The FV105 Sultan is the command vehicle member of the Scorpion/Scimitar family and is used by only one unit of a tracked Infantry battalion. This is the Platoon Headquarters of the Mortar Platoon within the Fire Support Company; the Platoon HQ has two Sultans. Very basically, the Sultan is similar to the Spartan but has a higher roof to provide more internal space for the many items used in the command role and for the various bodies and visitors who will have to be accommodated. To provide yet more working space there is a canvas penthouse that can be erected over the rear of the vehicle on bows and when not in use the penthouse is stowed either on the roof or on the front of the hull. Air conditioning is provided for the occupants and the armament is limited to a single L7A2 GPMG for local defence. Smoke dischargers are mounted on the front hull.

In some battalions Sultans might be encountered in use by other platoon HQs and perhaps even by the Battalion Commander in place of the more usual FV432 command variant.

FV107 Scimitar

Crew:	3
Weight in action:	7,756kg
Length, gun forward:	4.985m
Length of hull:	4.794m
Width:	2.235m
Height overall:	2.102m
Ground clearance:	0.356m
Track width:	432mm
Max road speed:	80.5km/hr
Road range:	644km
Fuel capacity:	423 litres
Gradient:	60%
Fording:	1.067m
Engine:	Jaguar J60 No 1 Mark 100B petrol developing 190bhp at 4,750rpm
Armament:	1×30mm L21A1 Rarden gun 1×7.62mm L37A1 machine gun

The FV107 Scimitar is a reconnaissance vehicle used within the tracked battalions by the Reconnaissance Platoons — each Recce Platoon has eight Scimitars, two with the Platoon Headquarters and two with each of the three Recce Sections.

The Scimitar is part of the CVR(T) family, a family that evolved from an Army requirement dating back to the early 1960s. In time the family grew to include the FV101 Scorpion with a 76mm gun, the Swingfire guided missile-armed FV102 Striker, the FV103 Spartan (qv), the FV104 Samaritan ambulance, the FV105 Sultan command vehicle (qv), the FV106 Samson recovery vehicle and the FV107 Scimitar. This family of tracked vehicles all use the same basic drive train, suspension and running gear and all are based on the use of aluminium hulls.

The Scimitar is very similar to the 76mm gun-armed Scorpion but is armed with the 30mm L21A1 Rarden gun. Both have turrets with a full 360° traverse while the Scimitar main armament can be elevated 35° and depressed to 10°. There is internal stowage for 165 30mm rounds. The crew comprises three men, with only the driver seated in the sloping front hull. The other two crew are seated in the turret. Internal space is somewhat limited so stowage boxes are usually located on the turret and hull rear.

The primary role of the Scimitar within the tracked battalions is reconnaissance and reporting enemy strengths and movements back to battalion headquarters. It is not intended for use as a combat vehicle pitted against enemy armour although it could have a useful role in knocking out opposing light armour such as armoured personnel carriers and soft-skin vehicles. The main gun also has a limited capability against low-flying aircraft and helicopters. Apart from reconnaissance the Scimitar can perform numerous roles within the Infantry battalion from keeping guard over obstacles to patrolling rear areas, for it is a versatile and handy vehicle. Infantry Scimitar crew members are trained by the Royal Armoured Corps (RAC) at Bovington and Lulworth.

FV721 Fox

Crew:	3
Weight in action:	6,386kg
Length, gun forward:	5.08m
Length of hull:	4.166m
Width:	2.134m

A Scimitar on a training exercise in Battlesbury Bowl on the edge of Salisbury Plain.

Height overall:	2.2m
Wheelbase:	2.464m
Ground clearance:	300mm
Track:	1.753m
Max road speed:	104km/hr
Road range:	434km
Fuel capacity:	145.5 litres
Gradient:	58%
Fording:	1m
Engine:	Jaguar J60 No 1 Mk 100B petrol developing 190bhp at 4,000rpm
Armament:	1×30mm L21A1 Rarden gun 1×7.62mm L8A1 machine gun

The FV721 Fox had its origins in the same Army requirement that gave rise to the tracked FV101 Scorpion family of vehicles. It was originally intended to be the wheeled replacement for the Ferret scout car but that intention fell by the wayside as the Fox evolved into a 4×4 wheeled reconnaissance vehicle with a fairly substantial armament.

The Ferret design origins can still be detected in the Fox but these are now overshadowed by the two-man turret that is similar to, but not identical with, that of the FV107 Scimitar (for instance the Fox turret can accommodate only 99 30mm rounds). Within the Infantry battalions, the two vehicles share the same reconnaissance role with the Fox used by the four two-vehicle sections of the Reconnaissance Platoon within the Mechanised (Wheeled) Infantry Battalions.

Using wheels and a 4×4 drive configuration in place of tracks, the cross-country capability of the Fox is somewhat less than that of the Scimitar but on roads it is much faster and less tiring to travel in. Otherwise there is little to choose between the two vehicles as far as their basic function is concerned. In the past there have been several unfortunate accidents caused by the propensity of the Fox to become top-heavy and topple under certain circumstances, but driver training can overcome this difficulty. The FV721 Fox was produced by Royal Ordnance, Leeds.

The Ferrets
(Data for FV701 [H])

Crew:	2
Weight in action:	4,395kg
Length:	3.835m
Width:	1.905m
Height:	1.879m
Ground clearance:	330mm
Max road speed:	93km/h
Range:	300km
Fuel capacity:	96 litres
Gradient:	46%

Fording:	0.914m
Engine:	Rolls-Royce B60 Mk 6A petrol developing 129bhp at 3,750rpm
Armament:	1×7.62mm L7A2

Above:
A Fox on Salisbury Plain.

Below:
A Fox and a lightweight Land Rover patrolling the Berlin Wall.
Army Public Information, Berlin

The Ferret Scout Cars must rate as among the oldest armoured vehicles still in use by the Infantry and the Army in general. The first of them was produced in 1950 and although production was continued until 1971 most of the examples still in use today are now in the vintage class.

The Ferret was based on the WW2 Daimler Scout Car and the two vehicles have many recognition points in common. Over the years many Ferret variants have been produced but one of the most commonly-encountered variants still in use is the FV701 (H), originally the Mk 2/3. This is an open 4×4 vehicle with an open top to the crew compartment which contains the driver (using a steering wheel with an odd rearward slant) and the commander. Armament is limited to a L7A2 machine gun at best and for many operations even this is not carried. Overhead protection is limited to a canvas screen to keep out the worst of the weather. Some versions still in use have a small turret in which case the crew might be increased to three.

The Ferret is retained as a general liaison vehicle within the Infantry battalions based in Germany. The user is the Battalion 2 IC who uses the Ferret to liaise with units within a battalion. More Ferrets may be found in the Signals Platoon, in use by the Assault Pioneer Warrant Officer and by various sections in the Fire Support Company.

The Ferret is one of the vehicles due to be replaced as part of the Future Families of Light Armoured Vehicles (FFLAV) programme.

Below:
A Fox on the Lulworth Ranges.

Facing page, top:
A Ferret at speed.

Facing page, bottom:
The Infantry's main supply load carrier, the Bedford MK, is also used by many TA Infantry battalions as a personnel carrier.

Top:
A 1-tonne Land Rover in a typical military environment.

Above:
The Stalwart high mobility load carrier, due to be replaced in Infantry logistic units by the Bedford TM 4-4.

12 Weapons

The infantryman in the British Army of today is trained to a high standard of proficiency on a wide range of weapons, the details of which are outlined below.

Rifle 7.62mm L1A1

Calibre:	7.62mm
Weight loaded:	5.074kg
Length:	1,143mm
Length of barrel:	533.4mm
Magazine capacity:	20 rounds (30 rounds optional)
Muzzle velocity:	838m/sec
Rate of fire (practical):	20rpm
Effective range:	up to 600m

At the time of writing the L1A1 rifle was still the standard rifle for most of the Infantry although it is in the process of being exchanged for the new 5.56mm L85A1 Individual Weapon (IW) with front line units.

The L1A1 has been the standard rifle of the British Army for over 20 years. It replaced the old Lee-Enfield 0.303in No 4 Mk 1 bolt action rifle and its origins were Belgian. The weapon from which the L1A1 originated was the Fabrique Nationale (FN) Fusil Automatique Legere, or FAL. The Belgian FAL was (and still is) one of the most widely used of postwar rifle designs but in its original form it had a fully automatic fire mode. This was one feature that was designed out for the 'British' version as the L1A1 fires semi-automatically, ie single shot only. Other

Left:
A soldier of the Black Watch on duty in Northern Ireland armed with a L1A1 SLR equipped with a SUIT sight. *MoD*

alterations were made to suit British requirements and production was carried out at the then Royal Ordnance Factory at Fazakerly and the Royal Small Arms Factory (now Royal Ordnance, Small Arms Division) at Enfield Lock in Middlesex.

The L1A1 is a gas operated weapon with propellant gas tapped off from the barrel (under the foresight) driving a piston system to unlock the breech block and produce all the loading and spent case ejection actions. Rounds are fed from a 20-round box magazine under the receiver (the 30-round magazine used with the L4A4 machine gun can also be employed). Magazines may be filled using a special filler device although rounds can be loaded into the magazine lips quite rapidly by hand action only.

The protruding barrel is a distinctive feature of the L1A1 carried over from the FAL and the muzzle is fitted with a combined flash hider and rifle grenade launcher. (No rifle grenades are currently in service and have not been used by the British Army for many years.) The muzzle is also the locating point for the L1A3 or L1A4 bayonet (using a spring catch) and the L6A1 or L1A2 blank

Below:
The 5.56mm L85A1 Individual Weapon (IW).
Royal Ordnance

firing attachment. A folding-down carrying handle is provided.

The fixed sights are of the 'iron' aperture rearsight and blade foresight type and are calibrated for ranges between 200 and 600m. However the rifle is often employed with the L1A1 or L1A2 Sight Unit Infantry Trilux or SUIT sight, an optical sight unit with an inverted aiming post used to obtain a rapid aim at most combat ranges. The Infantry Weapons Sight (IWS) L1A2 night sight can also be fitted to the L1A1.

Early production versions of the L1A1 were fitted with wooden furniture for the butt and forestock but this was later changed to black nylonite. Four butt plates of varying depth are available to adapt the butt length to suit individual users.

Rounds fired by the L1A1 are 7.62mm $\times$ 51 standard NATO. The following types may be encountered and are used by other British Army 7.62mm calibre weapons as well:

Round 7.62mm Ball L2A2 — standard round
Round 7.62mm Ball Target L2A2 — 'Green Spot' for sniper or target use
Round 7.62mm Ball L11A1 — produced by Raufoss of Norway
Round 7.62mm Tracer L5A3 — red tip to bullet, not normally used with the L1A1
Round 7.62mm Short Range L14A1 — plastic bullet, little used

Round 7.62mm Blank L13A1 — crimped case with no bullet

Round 7.62mm Drill L1A2 — inert with red grooved case

Round 7.62mm Inspection L3A1 — inert round for use by armourers, silver case

The Sparten training round, using a low power propellant charge and a frangible plastic bullet, is under development. One further accessory is the 0.22in Conversion Set L12A1 that converts a standard weapon for low cost firing on indoor or short training ranges.

When the L1A1 first entered service it was the cause of a great deal of criticism from conservative soldiers, usually on the grounds of its lack of accuracy at long ranges compared to the old Lee-Enfield. Over the years the L1A1 proved itself to be a satisfactory weapon that has provided good service and now that the IW is in the offing the L1A1 is all of a sudden one of the finest Infantry weapons ever designed! It will be around for years to come.

5.56mm Individual Weapon L85A1

Calibre:	5.56mm
Weight loaded:	4.98kg
Length:	785mm
Length of barrel:	518mm
Magazine capacity:	30 rounds
Muzzle velocity:	940m/sec
Rate of fire (cyclic):	650-800rpm
Effective range:	up to 400m

The British Army was an early advocate of the use of small rifle calibres and their first attempt to move away from over-powerful long range cartridges was made before the Great War. That project was terminated by the events of 1914 and it was the late 1940s before another attempt could be made. A new 0.280in cartridge was designed and rifles were produced to fire it, the best known being the ill-fated EM2. Again the project was terminated, this time by the politically-enforced adoption of the American 7.62mm × 51 round that became the NATO standard. While the NATO round is a good all-rounder, it is really too powerful for Infantry rifles so the many attempts to design 7.62mm assault rifles capable of producing useful volumes of automatic fire which can be delivered with any degree of accuracy have largely come to naught.

Above:
LA85A1 IWs with magazines removed.

Thus the L1A1 was selected and adapted to fire single shots only at a time when other users were thinking in terms of fully automatic rifle fire. For a while the idea of a British small calibre rifle lapsed only to be revived again during the early 1970s with the design of a new 4.85mm cartridge, the result of a long period of development that at one time involved a 6.25mm × 43 round (among others). A new rifle known as the XL64E5 was developed (a version known as the XL68E2 was produced for left-handed users) to fire the 4.85mm round and the rifle and cartridge combination was entered in a series of trials intended to determine a new standard NATO cartridge.

The trials were made necessary by the United States armed forces abandoning their over-powerful 7.62mm × 51 cartridge in favour of a smaller 5.56mm × 45 round (the M193), and by so doing emphasising the correctness of the British small-calibre approach to Infantry small arm calibres. The outcome of the NATO trials was a Belgian

variation (the SS109) of the American 5.56mm round, so further development of the British 4.85mm cartridge was terminated.

But all was not lost. The British 4.85mm cartridge was designed using a 5.56mm × 45 case and the overall form of the XL64E5 was taken as the starting point for the combat rifle design to replace the L1A1. After a great deal of development involving an interim model known as the XL70E3, plus a few production hiccups, the 5.56mm Individual Weapon (IW) L85A1 is now in service with the Infantry.

The IW is one component in a family of weapons known as the Enfield Weapon System or SA80, the other component being the L86A1 Light Support Weapon or LSW (qv). Both weapons have much in common, the most obvious design feature being the 'bullpup' layout with the magazine located behind the trigger group. This makes the IW a compact weapon that is easily handled and stowed within the confines of armoured personnel carriers and helicopters where the modern combat soldier spends much of his 'working' time.

The design of the L85A1 is 'all in line' with the butt, action and barrel in a straight layout. The main body is manufactured from pressed steel. Gas operation is used for the action, employing the rotary bolt-head locking system found in many other recent small arms designs. Using the relatively low-powered 5.56mm × 45 cartridge means that the L85A1 can be fired on full automatic without the recoil forces making the weapon unmanageable. The fire selection lever can be set to either automatic or self-loading single shot fire — the usual safety catch is also provided. Firing is from a closed bolt in both fire modes.

The weapon layout means that the sighting system has to be raised above the level of the receiver to accommodate the user's aiming eye, and the Infantry version of the L85A1 uses a SUIT sight variant known as the SUSAT (Sight Unit Small Arms Trilux) L9A1. This has a ×4 magnification and can be used as a surveillance and weapon aiming unit in reduced light conditions. The sight has the advantage that it raises the marksmanship of the average soldier considerably for the simple reason that he is better able to see his target, especially under poor lighting conditions or against dark backgrounds. The SUSAT is expensive so only the Infantry will be issued with it — other IW users will be

Far left:
The L85A1 being fired from the kneeling position.

Left:
L85A1 complete with bayonet.

issued with 'iron' sights that have the rearsight incorporated into a carrying handle fitted in place of the SUSAT; the blade foresight will be located on a post over the high impact nylon forestock.

The L85A1 is issued with a stainless steel bayonet that is something of a design marvel in its own right. It can be used as a combat knife as well as a bayonet and in conjunction with its scabbard it can serve as a wire cutter. The scabbard also incorporates a saw blade, a bottle opener and a sharpening stone. The hollow bayonet handle fits over a muzzle flash hider that can also be used to fire rifle grenades, should they ever come back into British Army use.

The makers of the L85A1 are Royal Ordnance, Small Arms Division, at Enfield Lock in Middlesex; production will eventually switch to Royal Ordnance, Nottingham. They use the commercial name of Endeavour for the weapon but to the soldier it is the IW or L85A1. Each rifle is issued with two canvas tool rolls containing cleaning gear, a multi-purpose stripping and maintenance tool and a few spare parts. Accessories include a blank firing attachment, a plastic muzzle cap to keep out dirt, and a sling. A 0.22in training adaptor is available. The Snipe image intensifier sight can be fitted in place of the SUSAT when the L85A1 is used at night or under poor lighting conditions.

The 30-round box magazine is made of light alloy and has the same interface as the widely-used American M16 magazine. Extra magazines are taken into action ready-loaded (from 10-round chargers) and carried in pouches. Rounds available include ball, tracer, blank and drill and a low power training round known as the Sparten is under development.

The L85A1 is suitable for right-hand users only but left-handers can be trained to use the weapon effectively. Perhaps the most far-reaching handling feature of the IW is that its compact length meant that a new form of arms drill had to be devised for occasions when the weapon is carried on parade.

The main advantage of the IW for the soldier is that it provides him with a considerably larger fire-power potential compared to earlier weapons. The ability to fire automatic bursts means that each Infantry section can now deliver a greater amount of fire-power when required and yet the use of a smaller and lighter cartridge means that each individual can carry more rounds for immediate use than before. This combination

Above:
A soldier of the Duke of Edinburgh's Royal Regiment in Crossmaglen, South Armagh, armed with a 5.56mm M16.
HQ Northern Ireland Public Relations

will make a considerable impact on future Infantry tactics.

Rifle 5.56mm M16

Calibre:	5.56mm
Weight loaded (30-round magazine):	3.73kg
Length:	990mm
Length of barrel:	508mm
Magazine capacity:	20 or 30 rounds
Muzzle velocity:	1000m/sec
Rate of fire (cyclic):	700-950rpm
Effective range:	up to 400m

When the American Armalite AR-15 5.56mm rifle appeared on the scene in the early 1960s, it appeared to be just the form of small-calibre Infantry weapon that the British Army had been seeking for some time. Almost as soon as the AR-15 was marketed the British Army ordered an evaluation batch which was soon followed by a larger order for what has been reported as 10,000 examples. It should be noted that this batch was ordered before the US Army adopted the AR-15 as their M16 rifle.

The M16 has never been adopted as a front-line weapon by the British but it has been extensively used in theatres such as Belize, the Far East and even Northern Ireland — the weapon has also been a great favourite with the Royal Marines. The M16 has proved to be light and handy, but it was never deemed suitable for large-scale use and has been used for familiarisation with the small calibre rifle concept and for the development of suitable tactics and fire control drills commensurate with each man having a fully automatic fire weapon. Once the IW is fully issued the M16s will be withdrawn.

It should be noted that the bulk of the AR-15/M16s used by the Army are of the original M16 pattern and lack the bolt closure plunger fitted to the later M16A1 introduced by the US Army after combat experience in Vietnam. The M16 is a gas operated weapon, using the same rotary bolt head lock employed on the IW, and overall the emphasis is on ease of production. Much use is made of mouldings and plastic materials where possible. The result is a light weapon that does not appear to last very well under arduous use, despite the overall high standard of finish. Most M16s now in Army service show signs of wear and tear, but never to the point of being unserviceable.

The AR-15/M16 fires the M193 5.56mm×45 cartridge which is available in several forms including ball, tracer, blank, drill and so on. Box magazines holding 20 or 30 rounds are available with the most favoured being the slightly curved 30-round variant.

The 5.56mm ball round has been the subject of a great deal of controversy for a variety of reasons, one being its lack of power at long range (for which it was not designed) and another the dreadful wounds it can inflict under certain conditions. It should be stressed that the M193 cartridge was designed for use at combat ranges up to about 400m and is in no way a long range cartridge. At most combat ranges its combination of muzzle velocity and muzzle energy makes it more than efficient.

Extras for the M16 include a blank firing muzzle attachment, a bayonet and a sling. The M16 can be used with the M203 40mm grenade launcher which clips under the forestock. A number of these have been obtained by the Army for familiarisation and special purpose employment.

Rifle 7.62mm L42A1

Calibre:	7.62mm
Weight complete:	5.56kg
Length:	1,181mm
Length of barrel:	701mm
Magazine capacity:	10 rounds
Muzzle velocity:	838m/sec
Rate of fire:	single shot
Effective range:	1,000m plus

When the 7.62mm L1A1 rifle entered service, it was apparent that it lacked the accuracy required for a sniper rifle, so a number of Lee-Enfield 0.303in bolt action rifles were converted to the new 7.62mm calibre and retained in use. The rifles used for the conversion were either the Rifle No 4 Mk 1(T) or Mk 1*(T), and as well as fitting new heavy barrels the opportunity was taken to revise the wooden furniture to keep the weight down and make some alterations to the trigger mechanism, plus some other slight changes. A new magazine was also introduced to suit the shape of the new rimless cartridge. The resultant weapon, the Rifle 7.62mm L42A1, has been in service since 1970 and has repeatedly proved to be a very accurate weapon. It has now been largely replaced by the L97A1, but no doubt some will remain around for some time to come.

The sighting device used on the L42A1 is the L1A1 telescope, a conversion of the old No 32 Mk 3. The sight mount is calibrated for ranges up to 1,300m although the maximum effective range, even in the hands of a skilled marksman, is usually limited to around 1,000m. A special sniper's sling is used when aiming the rifle and when not in use the weapon is kept in a fitted wooden chest along with all its accessories.

The usual ammunition used with the L42A1 is the Radway Green-produced Round 7.62mm Ball Target L2A2, the 'Green Spot' ammunition. Rounds from selected batches are used, and they are usually fed into the bolt action one at a time by hand, leaving a full magazine ready for emergencies.

Another conversion of the old Lee-Enfield 0.303in rifle is the L39A1. This is not a combat weapon as it is used for contest target shooting and is fitted with special 'iron' target sights.

The 7.62mm L42A1 sniper rifle.

7.62mm Rifle L97A1

Calibre:	7.62mm
Weight:	6.5kg
Length:	adjustable 1,124-1,194mm
Length of barrel:	655mm
Magazine capacity:	10 rounds
Muzzle velocity:	838m/s
Rate of fire:	single shot
Effective range:	1,000m

Good as the L42A1 was as a sniper rifle, it was the product of a bygone design era. Recent technological advances in the field of rifle design are such that the old L42A1 is no longer as accurate as more recent models. Thus, when the Infantry began to look for a L42A1 replacement, they specified a standard of accuracy involving a first-round hit at 600m and accurate harassing fire out to 1,000m. A shoot-out contest between several sniper rifle designs was held from late 1984 to early 1985 and the successful entry was a product of Accuracy International Ltd who are based at Portsmouth.

Their entry is now the L97A1. It is the 'Infantry' version of the Model PM rifle, a

Above:
The Accuracy International 7.62mm L97A1 sniper rifle, the replacement for the L42A1.
Accuracy International

custom-built design using the Mauser front-locking bolt action as a basis, but allied to a number of novel design features. The bolt action has a handle that is designed to be manually operated with a minimum of user effort and movement, and is so arranged that the user does not have to remove his eye from the sights as it reciprocates. The trigger mechanism is of the usual two-stage type that can be removed entirely from the rifle and used in another if required. The furniture is made from a tough olive green plastic bolted on to an aluminium 'chassis' and is so arranged that the forestock does not touch the heavy floating barrel at any point. The forestock is provided with a light and

Below:
A Barenar telescope, the new sniper's spotting telescope that will eventually replace the old brass spotting and scout telescopes that have been in use since WW1. The Barenar will be used in conjunction with the L97A1.

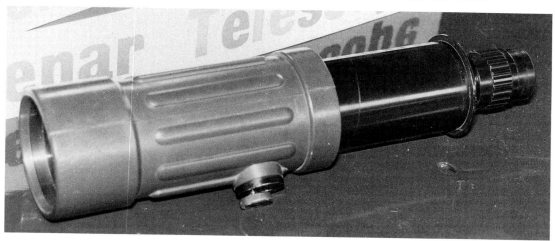

Above:
A 7.62mm L7A2 machine gun in its GPMG(SF) configuration. *Royal Ordnance*

7.62mm General Purpose Machine Gun L7A2

Calibre:	7.62mm
Weight loaded (LMG):	13.85kg
Weight of tripod:	13.64kg
Length (LMG):	1,232mm
Length (HMG):	1,049mm
Length of barrel:	629mm
Type of feed:	50 or 100-round belts
Muzzle velocity:	838m/sec
Rate of fire (cyclic):	625-750rpm
Rate of fire, practical, LMG:	100rpm
Rate of fire, practical, HMG:	200rpm
Effective range, LMG:	800m
Effective range, HMG:	1,800m plus

adjustable folding bipod to steady the aim and to keep the weapon pointed at a target for prolonged periods without undue user fatigue.

The L97A1 is equipped with fixed sights for use out to 600m but is more usually aimed with a Schmidt & Bender 6×42 optical sight. It is also possible to fit various types of night sights. The butt can be adjusted in length by adding or subtracting plastic spacers behind the rubber butt pad. A sling can be fitted. When not in use the L97A1 is carried in a specially-fitted padded gun case that has a harness to allow it to be carried on the back. The case has fitted pockets and pouches to carry ammunition and accessories and is waterproof.

A special version of the L97A1 is fitted with a 'moderated' barrel (ie a form of silencer) which is used in conjunction with special subsonic ammunition. Range is limited to 250m at best and no fixed sights are fitted — only the telescopic sight is used. This moderated version is intended for use by special forces only.

Most Infantry battalions contain at least four sniper teams. Each team consists of two men, one using the rifle and the other acting as an observer and lookout.

The L7A2 machine gun fits into the category of weapons known as General Purpose Machine Guns, usually referred to as GPMGs or 'Jimpies'. This means that when fitted with a light bipod they can be carried and fired by one man and used as a light machine gun (LMG), while the same weapon mounted on a heavy tripod can deliver sustained automatic fire as a heavy machine gun (HMG). Barrel cooling is carried out by rapidly changing the air-cooled barrel in both forms.

The GPMG is a German design concept dating from before World War 2. The L7A2

Above:
Setting up a L7A2 GPMG(SF) on the Warminster ranges; the gun is not yet loaded.

had its origins in a Belgian weapon, the Fabrique Nationale (FN) Mitrailleuse d'Appui General (MAG) — a design that rejected many of the stamping and welding manufacturing expediencies evolved during World War 2 and instead used the time-honoured method of machining almost every part from solid metal. The result is a very sturdy weapon capable of absorbing the knocks of hard use but one which is rather heavy. In fact the MAG, and the L7A2, falls between two stools. It is really too heavy and awkward to carry as a LMG yet is unable to deliver the prolonged sustained automatic fire of the old water-cooled HMGs.

These drawbacks should not detract from the fact that the L7A2 has given good service ever since the type was adopted in 1958. As the weapon seems to be immune to wear and hard use many will remain around for years to come.

As a LMG the L7A2 is fitted with a butt and a folding bipod. As a HMG it is mounted on a buffered tripod (the Mounting Tripod L4A1) and the butt is removed; in this form it is known as the GPMG(SF) with the (SF) referring to 'sustained fire'. For long range or indirect HMG fire, the Sight Unit Trilux C2 can be fitted (this sight is also used on the 81mm mortar). The rapid barrel-change system is used when the barrel gets hot. When the L7A2 is fired in the GPMG(SF) role at least two men look after the weapon with one firing and another guiding the ammunition belts into the feed system; another man may observe the fall of shot. In the LMG role one man carries and serves the gun although other members of the section may carry extra ammunition belts.

The L7A2 is a gas operated weapon and an adjustable gas regulator can be used to ensure that the gun keeps firing under all conditions. Ammunition may be fed into the gun in 50 or 100-round metal-linked belts and a belt feed box is available. For firing blank ammunition a L3A1 blank firing muzzle attachment is used in conjunction with a special ammunition feed plate. The L1A3 muzzle cover is available to keep out dirt and each weapon is issued with a wallet containing some small spare parts.

Variants of the basic L7A2 are many but Infantry-associated models include the L46A1 — a drill and training version that cannot be fired — and the L37A1 which is a co-axial machine gun used on the FV107 Scimitar. The L37A1 is also used on the 'small turret' versions of the FV432. It has a special chrome-plated barrel which enables a larger proportion of tracer rounds than normal to be fired for aiming purposes without causing premature barrel wear.

The imminent advent of the L86A1 LSW (qv) does not imply the demise of the L7A2. While the LSW has replaced the L7A2 as the

Above:
L7A2 in the LMG configuration in action on the Suffield Ranges in Canada.

Left:
A L7A2 mounted on the commander's pintle on a FV432.

Below left:
The L7A2 Machine Gun mounted on a DESA mounting next to the commander's cupola on a Saxon APC.

The 7.62mm Machine Gun L4A4. *MoD*

section LMG, the L7A2 GPMG(SF) will continue to be used as a company support weapon. The L7A2 will also remain in use as an anti-aircraft weapon on many vehicles.

7.62mm Machine Gun L4A4

Calibre:	7.62mm
Weight loaded:	10.68kg
Length:	1,133mm
Length of barrel:	536mm
Magazine capacity:	30 rounds
Muzzle velocity:	823m/sec
Rate of fire (cyclic):	500-575rpm
Effective range:	up to 800m

The L4A4 will be familiar to many old soldiers, for it is the old World War 2 Bren Gun modernised to fire the NATO 7.62mm × 51 round. The L4A4 is no longer a front line Infantry weapon but it is included here as it is still issued to TA Infantry Home Defence battalions.

When the Mark 111 Bren was converted to become the L4A4 the opportunity was taken to fit a new chromium-plated barrel as well as other enforced changes such as a modified breech block and a revised box magazine profile. The new barrel now means that barrel changes in combat can be virtually eliminated and each gun is issued with just one barrel. Otherwise the old Bren Gun remains little changed and it is as reliable and as easy to maintain and use as ever.

5.56mm Light Support Weapon L86A1

Calibre:	5.56mm
Weight loaded:	6.88kg
Length:	900mm
Length of barrel:	646mm
Magazine capacity:	30 rounds
Muzzle velocity:	970m/sec
Rate of fire (cyclic):	700-850rpm
Effective range:	up to 1,000m

The L86A1 Light Support Weapon, or LSW, is the light machine gun counterpart to the L85A1 IW (qv) and thus part of the SA80 Enfield Weapon System (its commercial name is Engager). The LSW and IW share a common development cycle as the LSW was originally produced in 4.85mm calibre as the XL65A4. The XL73E2 was an interim 5.56mm model before the production L86A1 emerged.

The IW and LSW have about 80% component commonality and use identical mechanisms although the LSW fires from an open or closed bolt. The barrel of the LSW is longer and heavier than that of the IW, which improves accuracy, and a bipod is mounted on an extension under the barrel. The bipod mounting extension was added at a late stage of development when burst firing the XL73E2 was found to produce erratic target groupings. Fitting the bipod mounting extension, and the use of a grip under the butt for the firer's left hand, eliminated the problem and the L86A1 LSW can now be used to deliver accurate fire at ranges up to 1,000m. However, the lack of power of the

5.56mm × 45 cartridge at such distances means that the weapon is effective only to a lesser combat range.

This lack of combat range imposed by the ammunition is no disadvantage to the LSW for it is intended for use as a fire team weapon. Issue is at the rate of three IWs to one LSW so each Infantry section has two LSWs. Some argument exists as to whether the LSW is actually a viable light machine gun. It has only a limited ammunition capacity as it uses the same 30-round box magazine as the IW and sustained burst firing is thus not possible. This is just as well for the LSW barrel is fixed and cannot be rapidly changed. Perhaps the best definition of the LSW is that it is a 'machine rifle'. As with the IW, the LSW is produced by Royal Ordnance, Small Arms Division, at Enfield Lock; production will eventually switch to Royal Ordnance, Nottingham.

Machine Gun, Chain, 7.62mm L94A1

Calibre:	7.62mm
Weight unloaded:	17.86kg
Length, long barrel:	1,250mm
Length of barrel:	703mm

Type of feed:	disintegrating metal link belt
Muzzle velocity:	862m/sec
Rate of fire (cyclic):	520rpm @ 24V
Effective range:	600m plus

The L94A1 Chain Gun is a product of the McDonnell Douglas Helicopters Company (formerly Hughes Helicopter Inc) of Culver City, California, that is built in the United Kingdom (under licence) by Royal Ordnance, Small Arms Division. It is used on only one Infantry vehicle, the FV510 Warrior.

The Chain Gun is so called because its operating and feed mechanisms are powered not by the usual gas or recoil forces produced on firing but by an electrical motor driving an internal chain. It is the chain that actuates all the various moving parts so the mechanism operates quite independently of any ammunition quirks or problems, and the chain carries the load of dragging ammunition belts into the weapon. All mechanical timings can be made precise and consistently accurate, while misfires are simply elimi-

Below:
The 5.56mm L86A1 Light Support Weapon (LSW). *School of Infantry*

nated from the system. The motor and chain drive also has the advantage of being compact so when the L94A1 Chain Gun is used as a co-axial machine gun (as in the Warrior turret) it takes up minimal internal volume. There is also the advantage that the spent cartridge cases can be ejected forward and out of the turret along with the associated problems of spent propellant gases that could otherwise foul the atmosphere of the turret interior.

The L94A1 Chain Gun (maker's original designation EX-34) fires NATO standard 7.62mm × 51 ammunition fed into the weapon in disintegrating metal link belts of indeterminate length. The weapon can fire at its cyclic rate of 520 rounds per minute only 0.15sec after pressing the trigger.

There are two basic variants of the 7.62mm Chain Gun, differing in barrel lengths. The version with the longer barrel, described above, is for co-axial use. A shorter-barrelled version is intended for cupola and pintle mountings and for remote control applications. The short-barrel version is 660.4mm long and the barrel length is 580mm. It weighs 13.7kg.

Below:
The 7.62mm L94A1 Chain Gun which is fitted as the co-axial machine gun in the Warrior APC turret.

Ordnance Muzzle-Loading 81mm L16A2

Calibre:	81mm
Weight, complete in action:	37.94kg
Length of barrel:	1,280mm
Muzzle velocity (max):	297m/sec
Rate of fire:	up to 15rpm
Max range:	5,650m
Min range:	166m

During World War 2 the British Infantry suffered somewhat from enemy mortars and thereafter resolved never to get themselves in a position where their mortars were inferior in performance to those of their opponents. Thus, after 1945, a great deal of basic research into mortars and mortar projectiles was carried out at various Ministry establishments, including the then Royal Armament Research and Development Establishment at Fort Halstead in Kent, and some similar Canadian establishments. The end result was the 81mm mortar now known as the L16A2 and the degree of its success can be indicated by two examples. One is that the US Army has decided to adopt the L16A2 (in a slightly modified form known as the M252) and the other was a result of the 1982 Falkland Islands conflict. After that campaign some Argentinians stated publicly that the British

mortar fire was so effective that it could only have been achieved using body heat-seeking guidance heads fitted to the mortar bombs!

These two points emphasise how good the L16A2 is in design and other terms, but it should not be forgotten that any weapon is only as good as the men who use it.

The main component of the L16A2, the barrel, is made from a high-tensile nickel-chrome steel alloy and weighs 12.7kg. Its lower half is surrounded by heat-dissipating fins that allow the barrel to fire 15 bombs a minute for an indefinite period without producing over-heating (although the barrel will get rather hot in the process). The light alloy baseplate is manufactured using explosive moulding techniques and weighs 11.6kg. It allows a full 360° traverse without the need to rebed.

The mount, the Mounting 81mm Mortar L5A2, weighs 12.3kg and is of a type known as a 'k' mount due to its shape, an arrangement that allows levelling to be effected using only one of the two mounting legs. The sight unit, the C2, is a Canadian design and is located on the mounting. It weighs 1.25kg and is also used on the L7A2 GPMG(SF). A Trilux illuminating unit can be added for use at night.

The emphasis on component weight is made as the L16A2 is designed to be carried in three man-pack loads — they were man-carried during the Falklands campaign. Under more normal circumstances the weapon is carried in a Land Rover and dismounted for use. Using either method the mortar takes only a few minutes to set up and get into action. Mechanised (tracked) battalions carry mortars in specially-equipped FV432s. On these the mortar barrel is on a turntable mounting secured to the main compartment floor, with the barrel firing through the open roof hatch. Racks around the compartment walls carry up to 160 bombs ready for firing.

The 81mm calibre is a NATO standard so in theory it can fire virtually any NATO 81mm mortar bomb. In practice the weapon fires mainly British-produced ammunition, although the illuminating bomb is French, known to the British as the L39A1. Several types of high explosive (HE) bomb are in service including the L15A3 and the L36A2. The latter weighs 4.2kg and is an improved pattern with a revised body design intended to provide improved on-target fragmentation. The standard fuse is the point contact or delayed action L127A2, although others are available and a multi-function fuse is

The L16A2 81mm mortar.

under development. Bombs are fired using the Mk 4 six-element charge system which uses propellant cartridges added around the bomb tail to augment the primary cartridge in the tail base.

Each bomb is muzzle-loaded and allowed to fall down the barrel on to the fixed firing pin. As the bomb travels up the barrel a plastic obturating ring opens outwards from the bomb's widest point and effectively seals the gap between the barrel walls and the bomb. This prevents propellant gas from escaping (this is known as windage), a factor that could otherwise affect the weapon's accuracy, so the obturating ring is an important factor in the overall accuracy of the mortar system.

Other bombs include Smoke (white phosphorus) L40A1 and the reusable L27A1 Practice bomb with a range of only some 80m. Inert drill and training rounds are also available.

In recent years the old method of using firing tables and plotting boards for mortar fire control has been superseded by the arrival of the miniature electronic computer. The Infantry mortar teams now use a small hand-held computer known as Morzen for all mortar fire control tasks. It is easy to operate, can store sets of preselected target data for immediate use, and generally makes mortar fire control much simpler, more accurate and quicker.

Development of the L16A2 continues. At one time a programme to introduce new bombs with a potential range of over 6,000m was in progress, which would also involve improved propellants. One bomb that is currently under development is Merlin, intended for the top attack of armoured targets. Merlin is a terminally-guided armour-piercing bomb with an active millimetric-wave radar seeker in the nose. In-flight trajectory corrections are made using canard fins close to the nose. Merlin is considerably longer (900mm as opposed to the 483mm of the L36A2) and heavier (about 6kg) than a conventional mortar bomb so the range is understood to be limited to around 4,000m. Development is continuing.

51mm Mortar L10A1

Calibre:	51.25mm
Weight complete:	6.275kg
Length overall:	750mm
Length of barrel:	543mm
Muzzle velocity (HE):	103m/sec
Muzzle velocity (Ill):	127m/sec
Range (max):	800m
(min):	50m
Rate of fire (sustained):	3 bombs/min for 5min
(rapid):	8 bombs/min for 2min

The 51mm L10A1 light mortar has suffered from a protracted development life as its origins date back to the late 1960s when it was decided to replace the venerable 2in mortar, a weapon that dated back to before 1939 (some are still used for launching flares at training establishments). It was not until the very late 1970s that the weapon began to resemble its current production form, for early designs featured a monopod leg that was supposed to steady aim and thus produce greater accuracy. The monopod certainly did that but it kept breaking and by the time that problem was cured the designers learned that the Army never did require a monopod anyway and were quite happy to stabilise the mortar by hand, as they did with the old 2in mortar. The ammunition was also the subject of considerable development but the L10A1 mortar is now in production (by Royal Ordnance, Leeds) and in service.

The protracted development should not detract from the fact that the L10A1 is an excellent platoon weapon. It is very simple in concept being but a barrel on a small spade baseplate and with a Trilux illuminated ranging sight to determine elevation for firing. In detail the L10A1 is full of design finesse of all kinds, one safety feature being that double-loading is impossible as a second bomb will protrude rather obviously from the muzzle.

This is but one indication of the care taken in the design of the L10A1. Another is the ability of the mortar to fire bombs to ranges as short as 50m. This is achieved by the use of a device known as a short range insert (SRI). When this is introduced into the barrel it acts as an extension of the firing pin and takes up slightly less than half the internal length. Thus when a bomb is fired the space around the SRI acts as an internal expansion chamber that reduces the internal pressure. Bombs are thereby fired with a reduced muzzle velocity and a shorter range. When not in use the SRI clips on to the inside of the muzzle cap.

The back-pack for the 81mm L16A2 mortar barrel.

Above:
The new Merlin anti-armour guided bomb for the L16A2 81mm mortar. *British Aerospace*

Left:
The Morzen mortar fire control computer.

The L10A1 is held on its baseplate with the firer holding a webbing gaiter around the barrel. Bombs are allowed to fall down the tube and the barrel is aimed directionally using a white line painted along the barrel. The appropriate range angle is determined using the sight and the trigger lanyard is then pulled. This trigger system allows the mortar to be fired at almost horizontal angles for Infantry tasks such as house clearing and other urban warfare tactics.

Three types of bomb are available. The L1A1 high explosive bomb weighs 900gm and has an internal notched wire fragmentation coil to improve lethality. The usual fuse is the L127A2. To provide target illumination for the LAW 80 or other anti-armour weapons the L3A2 Illuminating bomb is used. This weighs 800gm, is limited in range to a maximum of 775m and burns for 44sec. A third bomb is the Smoke

Above:
The L9A1 51mm mortar.
Royal Ordnance

Screening L2A1 — it weighs 900gm. High explosive bombs are carried in a nylon fabric satchel containing five bombs. Smoke and Illuminating bombs are carried in satchels containing six bombs. Practice and drill bombs are also available. As an added bonus stocks of old 2in mortar bombs can be fired from the L10A1.

The L10A1 may be carried on a shoulder sling and each mortar is issued with a wallet containing cleaning gear and some spares. The usual rate of issue is one L10A1 to a platoon. In some battalions the weapon is carried and fired by a dedicated individual but in others this duty might be carried out in conjunction with some other platoon task.

40mm Grenade Launcher M79

Calibre:	40mm
Weight unloaded:	2.72kg
Weight loaded:	2.95kg
Length:	737mm
Length of barrel:	356mm
Magazine capacity:	single shot
Muzzle velocity:	76m/sec
Rate of fire:	6 to 10rpm

Max effective range:	
(area targets):	350m
(individual targets):	150m
Weight of grenade (HE M406):	0.227kg

The Army obtained slightly over 400 M79 grenade launchers from the United States during 1969 at the beginning of the current Northern Ireland Troubles and some are still held there although they do not appear to have been used in anger at any time. However the gradual toning down of the level of violence in the Province has meant that the M79s are no longer required there on the scale once anticipated so they are now used for training in locations such as Belize and Hong Kong.

The M79 is an American weapon that evolved from experience gained during the Korean War when conventional rifle grenades were found to have too short a range for many Infantry engagements. From this came the family of 40mm × 46SR grenades that can be fired from a number of special launchers. The M79 first appeared in 1956. The 40mm grenades employ an unusual propelling principle known as the 'high-low pressure system' that uses a two-compartment aluminium cartridge case. On

Left:
Loading the 51mm L10A1 light mortar.
Royal Ordnance

Above:
Bombs for the L10A1 51mm mortar; (from left) smoke, HE, illuminating, practice.

ignition propellant gases produce a high pressure within an internal chamber at the base of the cartridge case. This high pressure is allowed to leak through to the main low pressure chamber via carefully engineered vents where the resultant reduced gas pressure propels the grenade from the launcher. The propellant gases are released from the high pressure chamber at such a rate that recoil forces for the firer are also reduced. As the grenade is fired it spins to arm the grenade fuse once it has travelled about 14m from the launcher muzzle. Most 40mm grenades have a point impact fuse and with high explosive grenades (such as the M406) the lethal radius is about 5m. With some types of grenade the lethal radius is enhanced by metal pellets arranged around the main warhead charge of Composition B or RDX.

By contrast with the relative complexity of the 40mm grenade, the M79 is a simple weapon. The aluminium barrel is broken open in shotgun fashion and the grenades are loaded directly into the chamber. After the user takes a rather hunched stance to accommodate the odd-shaped butt, the grenade is fired by percussion. The slow and curved trajectory of the grenades in flight involves the use of an awkward sighting system, but trained users can place grenades with accuracy up to a range of about 150m. Maximum range is 400m.

In many quarters the M79 is now regarded as obsolete as it requires a dedicated user, ie the user cannot carry or fire a rifle or any other weapon while handling the M79. The advent of the M203 launcher which can be clipped under the forestock of the M16 rifle now does away with this dedicated user drawback and the Army has obtained small numbers of M203 launchers for trials and general evaluation pending the development of some possible future grenade launcher system for the Infantry. The M203 has its own trigger and quadrant sight system and fires the usual family of 40mm grenades to a maximum range of around 400m. Loaded weight of the M203 is approximately 1.67kg and it is 394mm long overall.

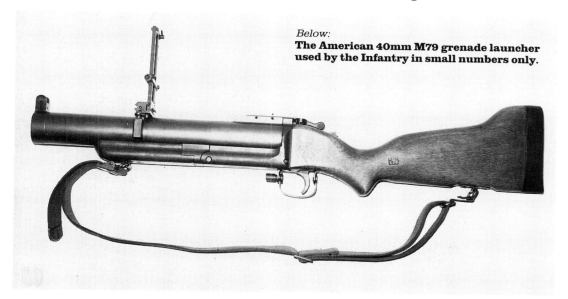

Below:
The American 40mm M79 grenade launcher used by the Infantry in small numbers only.

Assault Weapon

Few details of the proposed Assault Weapon for the Infantry can be provided for the simple reason that its form has not yet been determined. However, following combat experience gained during the 1982 Falkland Islands campaign, it has been recognised that the need exists for a weapon system that will close the existing fire support gap between Infantry units and the minimum safe artillery fire impact distance. What is required is some form of high explosive delivery system that will kill or incapacitate the occupants of an enemy trench or structure during the final and critical stages of an Infantry assault. The specification calls for a weapon that will employ soft launch (ie minimum recoil) to fire a projectile with a minimum calibre of between 50 to 60mm and an explosive payload sufficient to blow a man-sized hole in a wall or building. An alternative incendiary projectile is also thought necessary.

There is currently no such weapon in service anywhere (other than the cumbersome recoilless rifle with its many tactical drawbacks) so one will have to be developed. The nearest that any existing weapon concept comes to the Assault Weapon specification is the American Brunswick Corporation's RAW (Rifleman's Assault Weapon). The RAW system fires a 140mm spherical projectile from under the muzzle of a conventional rifle and although it is a powerful explosive payload carrier it is felt that it lacks the required accuracy. However the RAW concept may be used as the starting point for further Assault Weapon development.

Gun, Riot 1.5in L67A1

Although the L67A1 riot gun is not a combat weapon, it still forms part of the Infantry's inventory of weapons. It was developed as a projector to fire various forms of riot control munitions and was adopted for use mainly in Northern Ireland, where it has now replaced the array of similar projectors, mainly American in origin, that were hurriedly obtained when the present troubles commenced.

The L67A1 may be considered a progressive development of the Gun Riot 1.5in L48A1 and L48A2. The latter were originally signal pistols adapted to fire riot control munitions,

Above:
The L67A1 riot gun used in Northern Ireland.

but being smooth-bored they were not very accurate and lacked range. By contrast the L67A1 uses a longer rifled barrel, a rudimentary butt and a simple sighting system.

The range of riot control munitions available to the security forces in Northern Ireland is now considerable but not all are still in use. The range includes the following:

Smoke Screening L5A1 and L5A2
Smoke Screening L7A1 Green
Round Anti-riot 1.5in L5A3 (baton round)
Anti-riot Irritant L3A1
Anti-riot Irritant L6A1
Anti-riot Irritant L9
Anti-riot Irritant (Long Range) L11
Practice Anti-riot (Long Range) L14

There are plans to replace the L67A1 although it may be some time before a new projector is selected.

Milan

Missile	
Warhead diameter:	115mm
Mid-body diameter:	90mm

Wing span (wings unfolded):	265mm
Length:	769mm
Weight (ready to fire):	6.65kg
Weight of warhead:	2.98kg
Weight of warhead charge:	1.45kg
Velocity at launch:	754m/sec
Velocity at 2,000m:	200m/sec
Time of flight to max range:	13sec
Effective range:	25-2,000m

Launcher unit (folded)

Length:	900mm
Height:	650mm
Width:	420mm
Weight:	16.4kg
Traverse:	360°
Elevation:	up to 20°

Ammunition

Length:	1,260mm
Body diameter:	133mm
Weight (transported):	11.8kg
Weight (ready to fire):	11.3kg

Milan is the Infantry's main medium range anti-armour weapon. It is a second generation guided missile that relies upon a guidance system known as SACLOS (Semi-

Above:
The basic Milan Firing Post (FP). *MoD*

Automatic Command Line of Sight). This means that the firer simply has to keep his sight cross-hairs on the target and the missile guidance system automatically makes its own flight corrections to enable the missile to hit the target.

Milan stands for 'Missile d'Infantrie Leger Anti-char'. This immediately provides the prompt that Milan is an international system with its origins in a joint West German/ French venture that resulted in a consortium known as Euromissile to actually produce the Milan system. Milans are produced under licence in the United Kingdom by British Aerospace, Army Weapons Division, both for the Army and for export as Milan is now used by 35 countries. The Euromissile programme commenced as far back as 1962 and the first production examples were issued during 1975.

For most applications Milan is a one-man system although in action each launcher and guidance unit, known as a Firing Post (FP), has a second man who is used to provide support in the form of carrying extra missiles. Milan missiles are issued in factory-sealed container tubes that are clipped on to the launching unit. This unit consists of a

A Milan launcher complete with MIRA sight and showing a Milan rocket.

low tripod assembly and the guidance unit which is basically a periscopic optical sight containing the guidance circuitry. When emplaced the FP is small and inconspicuous and can be easily concealed from view on most types of battle terrain. The entire Milan system is very simple to use — it has to be for Milan is used by many of NATO's conscript-populated armed forces — and all operations can be learned easily.

Once the missile container is clipped on to the launcher it is ready for firing. On firing, the missile is propelled from its container by a piston powered by a gas generator at the base of the container tube (the same gas generator also pushes the spent container tube to the rear and off the launcher unit). After the missile has coasted forward for a short distance the two-stage rocket motor ignites. The delayed ignition avoids the danger of the rocket exhaust harming the firer and partially conceals the actual launch position.

Once the missile is under way, four small fins unfold from the missile body to provide spin for in-flight stabilisation and a two-

strand guidance wire unwinds from a tail bobbin. The wire is only 0.4mm thick and it carries signals for all in-flight trajectory corrections which are made automatically as long as the firer keeps the sight graticules on the target. To assist tracking of the missile as it travels towards its target there are infra-red flares in the missile tail.

Figures provided by the makers state that there is a 98% chance of a hit using the Milan at its maximum effective range of 2,000m. Practical results obtained from a series of 665 international test firings resulted in a hit probability of 88.6%. In addition to its use against armour, Milan has been fired in anger against helicopters (although not by the British Army) and during the 1982 Falkland Islands campaign some Milans were used very effectively against bunkers.

Milan has been the subject of considerable improvement ever since its introduction. One of the most obvious modifications has been to the shaped charge warhead (now known as the K115) which has been enlarged from an initial diameter of 103mm to the current 115mm to be able to defeat recent increases in tank armour. Under test and using a long stand-off probe on the missile nose, penetrations of up to 1,060mm of steel armour have been achieved. Another change has been the introduction of the MIRA thermal imaging

Above:
The LAW 80 in the firing position.
Hunting Engineering

sight which allows Milan to be used at its maximum effective range at night and under poor visibility conditions. MIRA adds an extra 8.5kg of weight to a FP and can be mounted on all standard launchers.

In Infantry battalions the Anti-Tank Platoon is divided into sections, each with five FPs. The FPs are carried in FV432s (in armoured and tracked battalions) and the two-man Milan teams dismount for firing. There is also a Mobile Section in Armoured and Mechanised (Tracked) Infantry battalions. This section carries its Milans in four FV103 Spartans equipped with a Milan Compact Turret (MCT) on the roof. Each MCT can carry two Milans ready to fire and the missiles can be fired and tracked from within the vehicle. To reload the commander has to leave his hatch and take fresh Milans from a crew member who leaves the vehicle through the rear door and hands up fresh Milan tubes. The Spartan interior has racks for eight Milans.

The eventual replacement for Milan is expected to once again come from an international programme, this time known as TRIGAT (Third Generation Anti-Tank). This is a two-part programme for the 1990s involving medium and long range missiles — the medium range missile will be the Milan replacement and will once again be developed by the Euromissile Dynamics Group. A full scale development contract was signed by France, West Germany and the United Kingdom during October 1987. Greece, Italy, Spain, the Netherlands and Belgium will probably join the programme later. It is anticipated that the medium range TRIGAT missile will use a 'fire-and-forget' guidance system and will employ tandem warheads to penetrate really thick tank armour, including applique armour of the latest types. It is also planned that the medium range TRIGAT will have an air defence capability against helicopters and low-flying attack aircraft.

LAW 80

Projectile diameter:	94mm
Launcher length (extended):	approx 1,500mm
Launcher length (closed):	approx 1,000mm
Weight when fired:	approx 9kg
Weight carried:	approx 10kg
Weight of projectile in launcher:	4.6kg

Effective range:	20-300m
Max range:	500m
Armour penetration:	in excess of 650mm

LAW 80 stands for Light Anti-armour Weapon 80 and it is the Infantry's main tool for defeating enemy armour at close ranges. It is intended to replace all other close range anti-armour weapons, not only with the Infantry but with all other combat and support elements of the Army.

LAW 80 has undergone a rather protracted development and pre-production period, but it has now been accepted by the Army and is in production. It is an unguided rocket system that can be carried and used by one man and it has an anti-armour performance that is understood to defeat armour thicknesses of more than 650mm. Exactly how a 94mm diameter shaped-charge warhead can achieve such a performance has understandably not been made widely known but it is believed that some form of shaped-charge design breakthrough has been made.

The LAW 80 rocket travels towards its target at a velocity approaching Mach 1 — wrap-around fins spring out after firing to impart spin and in-flight stability. The rocket is fired from a one-shot launcher tube constructed from filament-wound Kevlar and telescoped for storage and carrying. Each LAW 80 is factory-loaded and sealed, is handled in the same manner as any other piece of ammunition and it requires no pre-preparation from the firer before use other than removing the end covers and extending the launcher tube. If for any reason the weapon is not fired after opening it can be closed up for use on another occasion. LAW 80 has a shelf life of 10 years.

The sighting system of LAW 80 is rather unusual. It is based on a flip-up ×1 plastic reflex sight but aiming is checked by firing spotter rounds from an integral 9mm aiming rifle located under the main launcher tube. If the spotter round hits the target it produces an indicator flash for the firer. The main projectile can then be fired with confidence of obtaining a hit. The aiming rifle contains five rounds, considered sufficient for two possible engagements. After firing the launcher is discarded.

As LAW 80 is fired, the rocket exhaust produces a danger area in a cone about 20m deep to the rear of the launcher. The projectile is not armed until it has travelled 10-20m from the launcher and the rocket's propulsion element is fully spent before the projectile leaves the launcher. Safety measures include ensuring that the main projectile cannot be fired before the launcher is extended, the sight is in position and 'Arm' has been selected on the safety lever. Accuracy is stated to be of the order of 1mil from the point of aim.

For logistic purposes, LAW 80 can be delivered in a special LAW 80 Unit Load Container holding 24 weapons. It is possible to deliver this container by helicopter.

LAW 80 has been the subject of a great deal of detail design work headed by a team from the prime contractor, Hunting Engineering Ltd. Other concerns such as Royal Ordnance have also been involved and there is an extensive training package to accompany the introduction of LAW 80 into service. These include inert drill weapons, a classroom trainer and an outdoor range trainer that incorporates a fully-functioning spotter rifle while a sound generator is used to simulate firing the rocket. Once in full service LAW 80 will be a formidable anti-armour weapon.

Rocket 66mm HEAT L1A1

Calibre:	66mm
Length (extended):	893mm
Length (closed):	655mm
Length of rocket:	508mm
Weight complete:	2.37kg
Weight of rocket:	1kg
Muzzle velocity:	145m/sec
Max effective range:	300m

The Rocket 66mm HEAT L1A1 has for some time been regarded as (at best) obsolescent as it fires a rocket with a shaped charge warhead that can penetrate only up to about 300mm of armour, a performance imposed by the limitations of the warhead diameter. This means that the L1A1 rocket is unable to pierce the carapaces of most modern battle tanks so it is effective only against the relatively light armour of armoured personnel carriers and the like. The L1A1 also suffers from an overall lack of effective range for it can be used against moving targets up to 150m away at most. The maximum effective range of 300m is obtained only against stationary targets. Not surprisingly, the L1A1 is scheduled for replacement by LAW 80 but no doubt numbers of L1A1s will remain in use by some units for some while.

The L1A1 was originally the US Army M72 series HEAT (High Explosive Anti-Tank) rocket. Most of the British Army's examples

Above:
The L1A1 66m HEAT rocket in extended configuration ready for firing.

were produced under licence by Raufoss in Norway. Intended to be the successor to the old 3.5in 'Bazooka', the M72/L1A1 is a single-use disposable weapon that uses a telescopic launcher tube. Extending the tube causes the simple sights to flip up and also arms the firing mechanism. Once the rocket is fired it is stabilised in flight by tail fins that unfold from around the body. As always with such rocket weapons, there is a danger area to the rear of the launcher produced by the rocket motor exhaust as it is fired. This exhaust also has the tactical disadvantage of giving away the firing position.

For all its apparent disadvantages, the L1A1 is a weapon that is easy to carry and use. Apart from its intended use in the anti-armour role, it can also be effective against strongpoints such as bunkers. Normally the L1A1 is carried on a sling or tucked into webbing and when so carried it does not normally interfere with the use of other weapons such as a rifle.

Gun, 84mm Infantry L14A1

Calibre:	84mm
Length of barrel:	1,130mm
Weight complete:	16kg
Weight of round (HEAT L40A2):	2.59kg
Weight of HEAT projectile:	1.7kg
Muzzle velocity:	160m/sec
Rate of fire:	6rpm
Effective range (anti-tank stationary):	400m
Effective range (anti-tank static):	500m
Effective range (HE and smoke):	1,000m
Effective range (illuminating):	2,300m

Known as the 'Carl Gustav' in deference to its Swedish origins, the L14A1 is another anti-armour weapon that is scheduled to be replaced by LAW 80. The L14A1 has for some years been the main medium range anti-armour weapon of the Infantry and its passing will no doubt give rise to some misgivings. Unlike most other anti-armour weapons, the L14A1 can also fire very useful high explosive, smoke and illuminating projectiles that can provide the Infantry with a great deal of their own immediate fire support. Such portable firepower flexibility will no doubt be missed, for LAW 80 is an anti-armour weapon pure and simple.

From the viewpoint of the foot soldier, the passing of the L14A1 cannot come too soon. For all its assets the L14A1 is a heavy weapon to carry around (14.2kg) and as it is a shoulder-fired recoilless rifle the report produced on firing is stated to be 'less than enchanting', especially as the noise is produced only a fraction of an inch from the firer's ear. To use the L14A1 in action, two men are required — one for firing and the other for loading and carrying extra ammunition. More men might be involved in the carrying of yet more rounds. Another tactical drawback inherent in any recoilless rifle is that the area to the rear of the barrel can be rendered very dangerous to other troops as the weapon is fired. The back blast also kicks up highly visible clouds of dust or debris that can give away the firing position — a tactical factor that often renders the L14A1 a 'one shot' weapon.

In spite of all the drawbacks presented above, it must be emphasised that no weapon system is perfect and the L14A1 does possess many useful attributes. One already men-

Above:
A L14A1 84mm 'Carl Gustav' being offered for inspection by a Rifleman of the Royal Green Jackets.

Left:
An 81mm L14A1 with ammunition containers.

tioned is the flexibility provided by the range of ammunition available — even if the main projectile used is the L40A2 HEAT. When fired against armour inclined at an angle of 60°, this projectile can penetrate up to 228mm — against armour set at right angles this can be increased to about 400mm; both figures are still respectable and could inflict damage to many battle tanks. Accuracy is good and open sights or a ×2 telescopic sight can be used. Firing stability can be improved by using the weapon rest secured under the barrel — FV432s have provision for special resting bars across the top hatch for the L14A1 rest.

High explosive projectiles can find many uses against targets likely to be encountered by the Infantry and smoke has many tactical uses. Illuminating projectiles can be used to

light up targets for other weapons to engage. It is this aspect of the L14A1 that will no doubt be missed most.

But the ordinary soldier will no doubt disagree. For him, carrying and firing the noisy weapon is not a popular task. Even small-calibre range training with the various types of sub-calibre training devices available can produce a distinct ringing in the ears.

Cannon, 30mm Rarden L21A1

Calibre:	30mm
Length overall:	3,150mm
Length of barrel:	2,438mm
Weight:	110kg
Muzzle velocity (HE, APSE):	1,070m/sec
Muzzle velocity (APDS):	1,175m/sec
Rate of fire, cyclic:	up to 90rpm
Round weight (HE L13, APSE L5):	904g
Round weight (APDS L14):	837g
Projectile weight (HE L13, APSE L5):	357g
Projectile weight (APDS L14):	300g
Effective range:	up to 4,000m

Above:
A 30mm Rarden Gun fitted to a Scimitar CRV(T).

The L21A1 Rarden is used as the main armament of four types of Infantry combat vehicle — the FV510 Warrior, the FV107 Scimitar, the FV721 Fox and the FV432s of the Berlin Brigade fitted with Rarden turrets.

Design work on the Rarden commenced during the early 1960s with the intended target being armoured personnel carriers, low-flying aircraft and helicopters. From the outset, emphasis was given to accuracy, reliability, light weight, low trunnion loads and a small inboard volume. The selection of a 30mm calibre and the importance of accuracy has resulted in a weapon that fires automatically in short bursts only, as it was felt that fully automatic fire would degrade the potential accuracy of the weapon.

The result of this is that the L21A1 is something of an oddity among modern cannon in that it uses an ammunition feed involving three-round clips and a mechanism employing the long-recoil principle. Despite the name of the operating principle the mechanism takes up the minimum of space

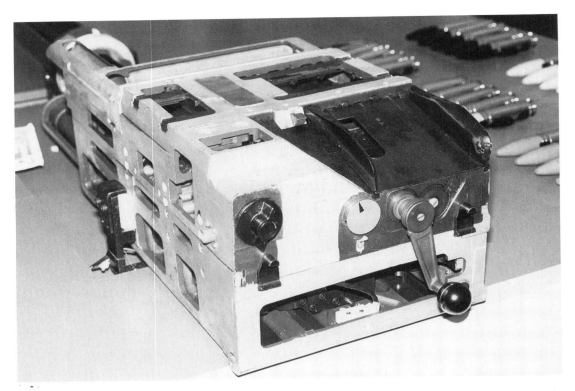

within a turret, while the use of the three-round clips limits automatic bursts, thereby maintaining accuracy of a high order — target groupings of 1m at 1,000m ranges have been recorded. Single shots can be selected. At any one time the Rarden can have six rounds ready to fire, five in the feedway and one in the chamber. The gun fires from a closed breech using an electrical solenoid — a mechanical firing system is provided for use in emergencies. All the mechanisms are enclosed within a casing and empty cases are ejected forwards out of the turret.

Ammunition fired by the Rarden is based on the Swiss Hispano Suiza (now Oerlikon-Buhrle) HS831L family. The L14 APDS (Armour Piercing Discarding Sabot) round was developed specially for the Rarden by Royal Ordnance and PATEC of California and this is now the main anti-armour projectile. It can penetrate 40mm of armour set at an angle of 45° at a range of over 1,500m. The other anti-armour round is the L5 APSE (Armour Piercing Secondary Effect) that is designed to detonate its hollow charge and release a pyrotechnic filling to create an incendiary effect inside the target's armour. A practice round (the L7 TP) is also available.

It should be stressed that the Rarden is not intended to attack the heavy armour of battle tanks. On all its vehicle applications the Rarden is intended for use against lightly-armoured targets and as such it is an excellent weapon.

Grenade, Hand-Rifle, Anti-Personnel L2A2

Weight:	395g
Length overall:	81mm
Max diameter:	60mm
Weight of explosive:	170g
Type of explosive:	55/45 RDX/TNT
Delay time:	4.4 ± 0.5s
Lethal radius:	10m
Number of fragments:	approx 1,200

The L2A2 grenade was based on the design of the American M26 grenade, but the British version differs mainly in having a separate

Above:
Fused (left) and unfused (right) L2A2 hand grenades.

fuse assembly — the lever-type L25A6. Despite the fact that the British Army has not used rifle grenades for some years the L2A2 was designed to be a dual purpose hand-rifle grenade. For the rifle role the grenade is fitted with a projector adaptor which is issued complete with a L1A2 grenade cartridge.

The ovoid body of the L2A2 is lined internally with a notched steel wire coil that breaks up into approximately 1,200 fragments on detonation of the main RDX/TNT charge. The fragments provide the main lethal potential of the grenade which extends over a 10m radius. The coil is 2.4mm in section and notched at intervals of 3.2mm.

For training there are the Grenade, Hand, Practice, Inert L3A1, L3A2 and L3A3. Also available is the Drill Grenade, Hand L4A1 and L4A2, both fitted with the Drill Fuse, Grenade, Percussion L30. The L2A2 replaced the No 36M hand grenade which is no longer used by the Infantry.

Smoke Grenades

Several types of smoke grenade are currently in use, the most common being the No 80 WP,

a canister-type grenade weighing approximately 550gm and filled with white phosphorus (WP). Originating from World War 2 years, the No 80 WP was also intended to be launched from various types of vehicle-mounted projector, but none of these remain in use. A new training screening smoke grenade has been developed.

A very similar grenade to the No 80 in use and appearance is the Smoke Screening Grenade L34A1 which weighs 308gm. It is 105mm long, 55mm in diameter and it uses a 'twist-and-pull' fuse system in place of the more conventional pin-and-lever type of the No 80 WP.

To provide coloured smoke for marking purposes the Grenade, Hand No 83 Smoke is still in service. Another WW2 veteran, the No 83 can provide red, blue, green or yellow smoke and the weight is about 500gm. Height is 140mm and diameter 63.5mm.

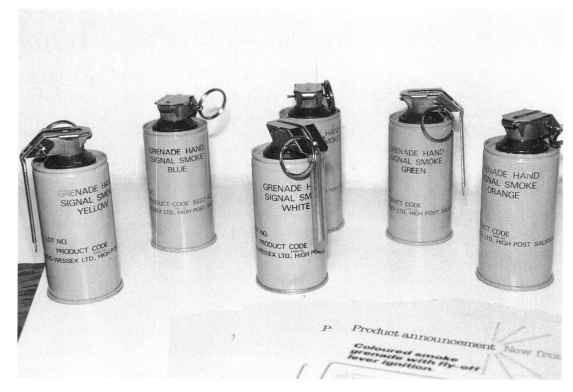

Above:
A selection of smoke grenades.

Anti-Personnel Mine M18A1

Weight:	1.58kg
Length:	216mm
Width:	35mm
Height:	83mm
Weight of main charge:	682g
Type of main charge:	Composition C-4
Range:	50m

The M18A1 mine is generally known as the Claymore mine, a name taken over from its American origins. The Infantry use the Claymore mine as an ambush weapon or to defend approaches to field positions and it is a remarkably effective and unpleasant weapon in both applications.

Basically, the M18A1 is a small curved plastic box holding a matrix of steel balls set into a bed of explosive. In use the mine is emplaced on four small scissor-type legs and the convex face of the mine is aimed towards its intended target area, using rudimentary sights on top of the mine body. Once emplaced, the mine is usually concealed in some fashion. As an enemy approaches the mine can be fired by remote control or by a tripwire. In either case, when fired the mine sends a lethal arc of steel ball projectiles over a 60° arc to a horizontal range of about 50m and an upward range of about 1m. Any person caught in that arc cannot escape injury or death for each M18A1 contains 700 steel balls.

The M18A1 can be just as dangerous to friendly forces as to an enemy for there is a danger area produced by blast that extends some 16m to the rear of the mine as it detonates. Careful siting of the mine is therefore necessary.

A single M18A1 mine is carried in a bandolier along with a firing device, wire, a simple test set and an electrical blasting cap. For training the inert M68 mine is available.

The replacement for the M18A1 was to have been the British-designed PADMINE, a fragmentation mine similar in concept to the M18A1. Development of this mine has been terminated.

13 Combat Uniforms

Few items of military equipment cause more concern to the soldier than his uniform. Not only is some form of uniform his working dress but it also marks him as a soldier — in a way it is his trade mark. He therefore takes an inordinate degree of interest in every facet of its appearance, form and efficiency for its intended role.

Military dress has evolved into a topic that had attracted an intense study that encompasses every aspect of its use — from where and when variations should be worn, to the design of military clothing for specific purposes. In the British Army the number and types of uniform are legion and are supposedly laid down by a series of complicated regulations that are usually observed only in the broadest terms. This does not mean that regulations are flouted for they are not — a form of uniform is strictly laid down and its terms have to be observed, but that does not mean that slight personal or unit variations cannot be introduced, for they are, on a bewildering scale.

These variations are most widely observed in the trappings of military dress — namely colours of clothing and formal uniform facings, badges and insignia and even variations in uniform style. Nearly every corps and regiment in the Army has these variations. They are jealously guarded for one reason or another and it is impossible to describe all these many and various shades of ceremonial and other attire in a book of this nature. Many books that set out to describe all the various dress and uniform variations used by the Army have been published, so the reader is directed towards them if an in-depth study of such matters is required.

What this chapter will attempt to do is describe in the very broadest terms the standard combat uniform worn by today's Infantry in the European theatre. It must be stressed from the outset that it can be a

The standard combat uniform as worn in 1987; the soldier is armed with the SA80 Individual Weapon.

description in the broadest terms only, for, as with more formal dress uniforms, combat clothing has many variations from the established form. There are many reasons for this, by no means least among them being the fact that at present the Infantry are in the throes of a re-equipment programme that involves not only weapons and equipment but clothing as well. As always, the complete transition from one standard to a new one cannot be made overnight, so at any one time some battalions will be wearing one form of clothing while the one next to them will be wearing similar but slightly different kit. These differences can also extend to a more personal level. Over the last few years many specialised commercial concerns have found it very profitable to market military clothing and equipment of all kinds and among their customers have been many serving soldiers. For one reason or another these soldiers have found it well worth their while to spend some of their pay on items of combat clothing and equipment to wear or use operationally, and in many cases such practices are condoned. One of the main reasons for this has been the introduction of new textiles that offer considerable advantages over in-service materials in terms of comfort, water-proofing or durability. It takes a considerable time for Service material-testing procedures to work their way through the mill, but in the meantime those same materials are often being offered commercially. Not surprisingly, the keen soldier will want to take advantage of such offers and the result is that in some battalions two soldiers can be encountered wearing apparently identical clothing made from two entirely different materials. In appearance they might be identical, but to the wearer they are very different. This purchase of commercial products can extend to equipment other than clothing. Webbing is always a popular purchase for the keen soldier, especially among TA battalions where the equipment

issued might not always be the most modern.

Another reason for variations in combat clothing and equipment is a purely economic one. Military clothing is usually manufactured from the best materials available at the time and produced to high standards of quality control. Such standards cost a lot of money and once a batch has been purchased it has to be used until it is no longer serviceable. That might take years in some cases, especially as most of the items involved are meant to last. In the meantime, as mentioned above, new materials or designs might be introduced but the soldier has to wear out his older kit before he can get the new. In such instances a purchase of the new kit is often made while the old is still serviceable.

To the untrained eye such combinations of commercial and issue gear can pass unnoticed but to the student of such matters, ie mainly the soldiers involved, such variations are important and can lead to all manner of personal uniform alterations. In some battalions such personally-introduced changes are strictly controlled while in others they are condoned if not actually encouraged. As long as a soldier is equipped in much the same manner as the next it matter little if his webbing belt is made of one material or another, as long as it is the same shade of camouflage colour. The same can apply to larger items of clothing for a combat jacket can be either the issue twill or Goretex as long as it follows the overall pattern and has the same and correct disruptive camouflage pattern and shades.

The importance given to these personally-introduced variations can be overstressed, especially as the changes introduced are relatively minor. The main overall uniform standards are carefully maintained and for much of his combat clothing the individual soldier can do little to change either appearance, design or the materials involved. This is particularly relevant to headgear, for while in combat the soldier wears a protective helmet. At most other times he wears a beret, now almost universally khaki although some regiments have their own variations of colour and in many cases the distinctive cap badge is further enhanced by the use of hackles or a coloured cloth backing.

The latest combat helmet is the No 6. This is a glass reinforced plastic helmet normally worn with a cloth cover over the top and with a band around it into which camouflage of one form or another can be inserted. The helmet is held in position with a prominent

chin-strap and has been designed to be used by airborne units as well as by the Infantry. The new helmet replaces the older and larger steel equivalent which is still likely to be encountered in use.

The basic combat uniform is formed from a windproof and waterproof smock and trouser outfit. These garments were originally issued in an olive drab shade but the latest issue has a disruptive pattern material (DPM) camouflage print in shades of olive drab, black, brown, green and buff. The jacket has an open fly front closed by a heavy duty zip fastener and buttons. The latest pattern of smock has some Velcro-type closures and has concertina-type pockets to permit extra stowage of items such as field dressings and personal effects. The trousers are gathered around the top of the boots by draw strings or heavy duty elastic bands and some battalions continue to add various forms of puttee-type wrappings.

The windproof and waterproof twill material currently in use for the smock and trousers is effective but has the disadvantage that it prevents loss of body heat, making prolonged wearing under exertion something of an effort. It also becomes rather heavy when wet. Newly-introduced materials can prevent both these drawbacks but are rather expensive so it seems likely that the present materials will continue in use for some time to come.

A hard-wearing flannel shirt is usually worn under the jacket and, beneath that, issue underwear can be of several types. For use in cold weather the latest issue is olive green thermal 'long johns' of the kind that can be purchased in High Street stores. At times an olive green woollen jersey known as a 'woolly pully' is worn over the shirt.

Under most circumstances the neck of the combat smock is worn open, as is the shirt. On many occasions the opportunity is taken to wear a camouflage netting scarf around the neck ready for immediate use, but in cold weather this might be replaced by a new issue item known as a 'head-over'. This is a form of woollen scarf that can be arranged to be worn over the head and ears.

The current all-weather protection garment in use is a waterproof poncho designed to be a multi-purpose garment that can be combined with others to form a rudimentary bivouac tent or even act as a simple stretcher in an emergency. Despite its various uses the poncho is to be replaced by a waterproof over-smock and trousers outfit. Again, for really cold weather, the over-smock will be provided with a padded inner jacket. To protect the hands the old woollen gloves have now been almost entirely replaced by black leather gloves with padded panels on the back and, in some cases, along the fingers. These gloves were originally designed for hand protection while on riot duties in Northern Ireland but have proved so popular that they are now a general issue. Wool continues to be used for issue socks but the latest form uses various other materials as well to increase durability.

That most personal item for the soldier, the boot, continues to be an item of contention. Experience gained in the Falklands in 1982 demonstrated that the old short ammunition boots with their direct moulded soles were of only limited use under damp conditions so the current high boot was developed. In their turn the issue high boot has also proved to be less than successful to the point where many soldiers have purchased commercial equivalents to overcome what are seen as deficiencies in the design. Consequently a new design of issue high boot is in the pipeline. These will be lighter, more flexible and will feature a lining. Thermal insoles are now worn under cold conditions.

These days NBC clothing is likely to be worn during combat as much as the standard clothing. For many years the issue NBC suit has been the Mk 111 consisting of an over-smock, with an integral hood, and trousers — all made from charcoal-cloth paper-based material coloured either olive green or mid-grey. Known as 'Noddy Suits', these NBC suits are far from comfortable to wear as body heat builds up inside them to create a sauna effect on the wearer. This is partly overcome in the Mk IV suit by the introduction of a zip fly front that can be opened to allow some degree of upper body ventilation when conditions allow. The Mk IV suit continues to use the same material as the Mk III but is finished in DMP camouflage. The Mk IV is also provided with pockets. (The Mk III has only a single chest-located pocket).

The NBC outfit is completed by disposable rubber gloves with a cotton inner glove, and charcoal-impregnated over-boots. The latter are rather clumsy to fit and wear but allow the wearer to retain his familiar boots.

Left:
A Mk 3 NBC 'Noddy' suit in use with a S6 respirator; the black box is a NAIAD chemical agent detector and alarm. *MoD*

Above:
(Left) a soldier with full PLC; (right) a soldier wearing the Mk 4 NBC suit complete with overboots and S10 respirator.

Special over-boots are provided for use with skis.

That leaves the respirator. Of all NBC items this is the most complex in design terms as it must permit the wearer to breathe safely, while excluding all possible harmful agents, and yet allow the wearer to continue to operate as efficiently as possible while using weapons and communications equipment. This is not an easy combination of features to produce but the British Army's respirators are better than most. For years the issue NBC respirator has been the S6 which features an external and replaceable filter canister and a very effective face seal around the periphery. This is now being supplemented by the S10, a more modern design that carries over many of the better features of the S6 but features extras such as provision for an internal microphone and a drinking device that connects to the standard water-bottle via a flexible tube. When worn, the S6 and S10 are covered by the smock hood worn over the head and under the helmet. When not in use the respirators are carried in a semi-flexible case worn on the belt and this case is now a virtual fixture for every combat soldier. A relative innovation is the charcoal cloth facelet that resembles a surgeon's face mask. This can be worn in place of the respirator when the danger of chemical attack is low or when chemical agent concentrations in the vicinity are of a low level. It is not a replacement for the respirator and provides only partial protection for the user.

Mention of the belt prompts mention of webbing generally. The current webbing is the '1958 Mk II WE' consisting of a belt to which are attached ammunition pouches, a shoulder yoke, water bottle and small pack. Extra pouches and a bayonet frog can be

Above:
Close-up of a complete PLC; it may be some years before the Infantry gets this equipment.

attached to the belt (along with the respirator case) and a folding entrenching tool is another potential attachment. The webbing is made from a synthetic material that resists water and the closures are nearly all high impact plastic 'quick-fit' devices.

This pattern of webbing equipment was to have been replaced by the Personal Load Carrier, or PLC, but for various reasons (mainly financial) this may not now happen for several years. The PLC was intended to be introduced along with SA80 as it has been custom-designed to go with the new weapons, but SA80 users will continue to use the 1958 pattern for the foreseeable future, even if SA80 magazines do look rather lost inside the 1958 pattern ammunition pouches. The PLC not only has ammunition pouches tailored for SA80 but also has a novel back harness system with a nylon mesh panel on to which several forms of back pack, a sleeping bag and 'kip mat' can be fitted. There is a basic large pack with two side packs and, by a system of fixtures, all three packs, two packs or only one can be carried on the PLC. There is also provision for carrying a three-part folding entrenching tool at the rear of the harness and numerous other variations can be introduced. When all parts of the PLC are worn they can be protected from the elements by a waterproof cover that unfolds over them all. However it may now be some time before soldiers can appreciate the virtues of the PLC.

The above is a basic outline only and covers only the type of combat uniforms likely to be worn in the European theatre. Troops serving in the Arctic or in the jungles of Belize and elsewhere are clothed accordingly and to a different scale.

One last item still worthy of mention is that there is now no difference between the combat clothing worn by officers and other ranks. When considering almost every other type of uniform worn there are distinct differences between those of officers and other ranks, but once combat clothing is adopted there is no difference at all and the similarity even extends to junior officers carrying the same weapons as the troops under their command. The only differences that might be discerned are rank badges, but these are often worn in a very low visibility form and are identifiable only at short range — they might not be visible at all once NBC clothing is donned. The introduction of rank and other identification badges for use under combat conditions was the subject of much discussion as these words were written.

14 A Glimpse into the Future

The bulk of this book has been devoted to describing how the modern Infantry is organised and equipped and how it operates at present. It is possible that by the time these words are read the usual churn of operational and equipment decisions may have rendered some of the comments and descriptions provided to a state of obsolesence. Such changes are inevitable in a combat organisation that is constantly attempting to keep abreast of any developments that might arise but even at the time of writing there were many new items of equipment in prospect or in the pipeline. Some of these are outlined below but a few of them may never see service due to a number of factors. One is that the reason for their proposed innovation might simply disappear or be at such a low priority that the efforts involved will not be worth the end result. Another much more likely reason is that, despite a definite requirement, the necessary funds will simply not be forthcoming — other requirements might be more pressing when it comes to the final decision. Yet another could be that a current requirement might be overtaken by events as newer or better products or techniques become available. Finally, there is that dreaded occurrence, the Defence Review that could lay all manner of carefully made plans and intentions low at the stroke of a pen.

For all this, it is possible to make a few forecasts of what the future might bring for the Infantry, especially in equipment terms. These days it can take years to get even the simplest item of equipment into service as the lengthy processes of operational analyses, proposals, requests for consideration, design, development, tendering, testing, operational testing and final production, plus all the interim stages and committees involved, are all put through the procurement mill. Thus some of the future items mentioned below were actually initiated some time ago. For example, the Falkland Islands campaign of 1982 was highly productive in operational analysis terms but some of the findings made in the aftermath of that conflict were still being processed in 1988.

For the Infantry no particular time can be said to be settled. That is true of the present, for a major re-equipment programme is under way, from the smallest item to the largest. In monetary importance and tactical impact two programmes stand out. They are the Warrior conversion programme and the issue of SA80. At the time of writing Warrior production was proceeding smoothly, as was the conversion training programme (see Chapter 9), while SA80, having negotiated its initial production problems, was being issued to Regular battalions on schedule. Once they are equipped, the rest of the Regular Army will follow, followed by the Ulster Defence Regiment (UDR) and only then will the TA get SA80.

On a slightly less exalted level, deliveries of the Saxon wheeled armoured personnel carriers continue. It seems unlikely that more than the 500 or so Saxons ordered for the Infantry will be obtained even though the TA Infantry battalions earmarked for BAOR could do with them. Nor will there be any

Right:
Carrying a NAIAD chemical agent alarm unit to a position remote from the main detector unit next to a Spartan. *Thorn EMI*

more Warriors once current orders have been fulfilled. Once again, a lack of funds for these costly vehicles is the main reason and this will mean that many of the existing FV432s will have to run on well in excess of their anticipated service lives.

Vehicles such as the FV432 cannot last forever. As it is unlikely that more Warriors will be procured, an entirely new vehicle is envisaged. At present it is no more than a project under the designation of Future Light 'A' Vehicle and as yet few details have emerged for the simple reason that few decisions have yet been taken. The general intention seems to be that any new vehicle will be a relatively simple, low cost, general purpose armoured carrier that can be readily adapted to several configurations to suit various roles. It seems likely that tracks will be involved and that some form of light-weight aluminium or low cost composite armour will be fitted. There is even a chance that the Infantry version of the proposed vehicle will be but one component of a whole new range known as the Future Families of Light Armoured Vehicles (FFLAV).

On the wheeled vehicle front the current Land Rover series will gradually be replaced by the later Series 2 Land Rovers. This has been happening since 1986, but it will be some time before the change-over is complete and by then the vehicles will be known by new names. The replacement for the current ½-tonne Land Rover will be the Land Rover 90, known as the Truck, Utility, Light. Its slightly larger counterpart, the ¾-tonne Land Rover, will be replaced by the Truck, Utility, Medium, known to the outside world as the Land Rover 110.

At the time of writing, a completely new class of light truck for the Army was scheduled. This is to be the Truck, Utility, Heavy — a 2-tonne 4×4 vehicle. A contest between two vehicles — the Reynolds-Boughton RB-44 and the Stonefield P500M — was held during 1986 and 1987 but at the time of writing no decision had been made and it was still possible that the entire project would be terminated.

There is also a requirement for a new 4-tonne truck, not only for the Infantry but for the Army as a whole. The current fleet of Bedford MKs is to be replaced by a new design from either Volvo (UK), Leyland-DAF or AWD Bedford. Again a 'drive-off' competition between the various submissions was held during 1987 and 1988 and at the time of writing there was no clear indication of what the result would be, other than that the resultant vehicle would be very like the existing Bedford MK in overall performance.

In 1987 the largest truck used by the Infantry was the Stalwart HMLC (High Mobility Load Carrier), a 6×6, 5-tonne truck with a remarkable all-terrain performance. The Stalwart was procured by the Army in some number at a time when defence funds were more freely available so features such as an amphibious capability could be included. The purchase of a cargo-carrying vehicle with a similar cross-country performance is extremely unlikely these days for the simple reason the unit cost would be astronomical. Instead the Stalwart is scheduled to be replaced by the 8-tonne Bedford TM 4-4, a more sedate vehicle all round.

Leaving vehicles aside, the Infantry has now entered the electronic age with new surveillance and target acquisition equipment. The Reconnaissance Sections of the Armoured Infantry battalions are to be issued with the Observer Thermal Imaging System (OTIS), that will enable them to observe targets in darkness or in poor visibility. Also in prospect is the smaller SPYGLASS thermal imager, a hand-held device to be used by the Reconnaissance Sections of battalions other than those equipped with Warrior. They will also be used by Mortar Fire Control (MFC) teams, combined with laser rangefinders. These equipments require a supply of clean cooling air so battalions will be issued with the Charging Equipment Pure Air (CEPA) which will either be towed on a trailer in Warrior, FV432 and Saxon battalions or on a skid mounting carried on a truck.

The mention of lasers in the previous paragraph prompts further mention of an Infantry requirement for eye protection against laser emissions. On any future battlefields, lasers will be in use on a large scale and any direct exposure of the human eye to a laser beam could result in temporary or even permanent blindness. Research into some form of protective goggles is currently under way.

Visual protection of a different sort involves camouflage systems for vehicles. A new Vehicle Concealment Set has been developed involving three different elements. One is a vehicle cover known as Thermal Camouflage Woodland (TCW) that screens the heat emitted by vehicles and thus prevents detection by thermal imagers. The TCW is laid over the vehicle concerned and has to be used in conjunction with a camouflage net, typically the new Mk 7 Woodland Net. This

The Land Rover 110 Truck Utility Medium, recognisable by the 'eyebrows' over the wheel arches.

net is held over the vehicle on the Camouflage Support System (CASS), a new lightweight system of fibreglass rods arranged over the vehicle to support netting on small 'mushroom' heads at the ends of the rods. Longer term plans call for some form of 'instant screen' system whereby netting or some other form of visual protection can be automatically erected over the carrier vehicle seconds after it has come to a halt.

On the communications side the relatively recent issue of Clansmen radio equipments means that the Infantry is now fully up-to-date and any eventual replacement is still at the Staff Target level. In the meantime the KIPLING on-line tactical data encryption system for sending secure data messages was due to enter service during 1988. Further in the future is the Battlefield Information and Command System (BICS). The latter is a computer-based automatic data processing and presentation system for use at Battle Group levels that enables commanders to have at their disposal a constantly updated and organised array of relevant combat data.

At present BICS is still at a very early concept stage of development.

A few new items are scheduled for the Assault Pioneers. The current range of combat engineering power tools is being generally improved and a new powered digging tool is planned at the rate of one per company. The only totally new item of engineer equipment planned for the Infantry is a man-portable assault footbridge. This will be about 24m long and will be made of light aluminium alloys. A small number (around 20) are planned for a central pool somewhere in West Germany from whence they will be drawn as and when required. In the meantime the materials for the latest 'split hairpin' battlefield underground shelters are already in supply dumps.

Clothing is a very personal item for the foot

Right:
Target acquisition and surveillance using an OTIS (Observer Thermal Imaging Sight) on the right and a laser rangefinder on the left; this combination is used by MFC teams.

soldier and as always the Infantry have several innovations planned for the next few years. The Mk 6 combat helmet is already on issue but the Personal Load Carrier (PLC) that was intended to enter service at the same time as SA80 has suffered a funding setback and may not be issued until at least 1992. This situation could still be altered for the PLC has been tailored closely to SA80 and a lack of it will be the cause of some inconvenience to the Infantry.

Boots are very much part and parcel of the Infantryman's way of life and a new Mk 2 high boot is planned. The original high boot has not been such the success that had been hoped for and among the changes intended with the Mk 2 are a better lining, a generally lighter weight and increased flexibility. Also on the footwear front all soldiers will be issued with training shoes by 1989 in an attempt to prevent lower limb injuries caused by too much running on roads in heavy rubber-soled boots.

For use when in the field a new sleeping bag known as a Sleeping Assembly was planned for troop trials during 1988. This will consist of a sleeping bag, a Goretex cover and a compression sack to reduce carrying volume.

For load carrying purposes a special manpack carrier has already been introduced. This is a back-mounted carrier frame on to which all manner of heavy man-pack loads such as support weapons, ammunition and batteries can be strapped.

For more specialised use it is hoped to be able to introduce a new form of Combat Body Armour. The project is still in an early phase and only a few guidelines have been issued. It is known that the armour will be in the form of a light (about 2.5kg) undergarment to be worn under combat clothing and that it is intended for protection against fragments only. All being well, initial troop trials of some possible designs will have been carried out by the end of 1988. While mentioning

classroom and outdoor trainer versions. For use as a Milan replacement the international Trigat missile programme is well under way (see entry under *Milan* in Chapter 12).

A new multi-role fuse for use with 81mm mortar bombs is to be introduced. This will reduce the number of types of fuse that have to be carried into action at present. There are also studies under way to investigate the introduction of a large mortar with a calibre of 120mm. Such a weapon, already in widespread use with many NATO armies, would provide the Infantry with an even greater degree of fire support than that currently provided by the 81mm L16A2. The exact form of this weapon (towed or self-propelled) has not yet been determined.

In addition to the array of offensive weapons mentioned above, less dramatic equipments are planned to enter service. These include new practice grenades, a new smoke generator pot, an improved pattern of thunderflash and new battlefield simulation pyrotechnics in general.

Simulation and training equipments feature high on the future requirements list, the most important of which are Direct Fire Weapons Effect Simulators (DEFWES) which could be in use by 1990. DEFWES encompasses all the weapons likely to be used within a Battle Group and by use of coded low-power lasers and receivers it will enable realistic Battle Group training to be undertaken without recourse to the unrealistic training measures that have to be used at present. Using DEFWES, a rifleman will be able to 'fire' his rifle at another soldier who will then know he has been hit by the production of an audible and visual signal from his receiver harness. But if the rifleman fires his rifle at a tank no result will ensue. The system is capable of numerous variations and its introduction is awaited with interest. In the meantime the single-level Small Arms Weapons Effect Simulator (SAWES) which works only at small arms levels is being modified to accommodate SA80.

For range work, an Automatic Marking System for small bore targets is under way, while for use with anti-armour weapons some form of radio-controlled or winch-driven target that can simulate a full sized moving armoured vehicle is required. There is also a need for some type of target that can be used repeatedly with the HEAT warheads used on Milan and other similar weapons.

Unfortunately low-priority requirements such as these are often overtaken by more urgent operational projects.

special protective clothing, the Mk 4 NBC protective suit with its disruptive pattern camouflage and zip front opening has been accepted for service and will be universally issued once existing Mk 3 suits have been used up in training. The all-round improved S10 NBC respirator with its integral microphone and very useful drinking device will gradually replace the existing S6.

In the weapons field, SA80 has already been mentioned. The SA80 bayonet is still being issued and it is planned to introduce a 0.22 conversion kit to allow low cost ammunition to be used for indoor range training. Also for training, the Sparten training round with its frangible projectile and low power propellant charge is still under development in both 5.56 and 7.62mm calibres. For combat use a Common Weapon Sight (CWS) for SA80 and other weapons is scheduled.

By the time this book is published LAW 80 will be in service. With it will come drill,

Appendix — Divisions and Battalions of the Infantry of the Line

The Scottish Division: The Castle, Edinburgh

1st Battalion The Royal Scots (The Royal Regiment) (RS): The Castle, Edinburgh.

1st Battalion The Royal Highland Fusiliers (Princess Margaret's Own Glasgow and Ayrshire Regiment) (RHF): Glasgow.

1st Battalion The King's Own Scottish Borderers (KOSB): Berwick-on-Tweed.

1st Battalion The Black Watch (Royal Highland Regiment) (BW): Perth.

1st Battalion The Queen's Own Highlanders (Seaforth and Camerons) (QO HLDRS): Inverness.

1st Battalion The Gordon Highlanders (GORDONS): Aberdeen.

1st Battalion The Argyll and Sutherland Highlanders (Princess Louise's) (A and SH): Stirling.

The Royal Scots.

The Royal Highland Fusiliers.

The King's Own Scottish Borderer

The Black Watch.

The Queen's Own Highlanders.

The Gordon Highlanders.

The Argyll and Sutherland Highlanders.

The Queen's Regiment.

The Royal Regiment of Fusiliers.

The Queen's Division: Bassingbourn Barracks, Royston, Herts

1st, 2nd and 3rd Battalions The Queen's Regiment (QUEENS): Canterbury.

1st, 2nd and 3rd Battalions The Royal Regiment of Fusiliers (RRF): Tower of London.

1st, 2nd and 3rd Battalions The Royal Anglian Regiment (R ANGLIAN): Bury St Edmunds.

The Royal Anglian Regiment.

The King's Own Royal Border Regiment.

The King's Regiment.

The Prince of Wales' Own Regiment of Yorkshire.

The Green Howards.

The Royal Irish Rangers.

The Queen's Lancashire Regiment.

The Duke of Wellington's Regiment.

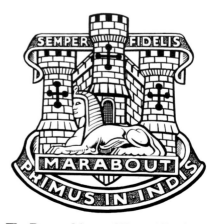

The Devonshire and Dorset Regiment.

The Cheshire Regiment.

The Royal Welch Fusiliers.

The Royal Regiment of Wales.

The Gloucestershire Regiment.

The Worcestershire and Sherwood Foresters.

The King's Division: Imphal Barracks, York

1st Battalion The King's Own Royal Border Regiment (KINGS OWN BORDER): Carlisle.

1st Battalion The King's Regiment (KINGS): Liverpool.

1st Battalion The Prince of Wales' Own Regiment of Yorkshire (PWO): York.

1st Battalion The Green Howards (Alexandra, Princess of Wales' Own Yorkshire Regiment) (GREEN HOWARDS): Richmond.

1st and 2nd Battalions The Royal Irish Rangers (27th [Inniskilling] 83rd and 87th) (R IRISH): Belfast.

1st Battalion The Queen's Lancashire Regiment (QLR): Preston.

1st Battalion The Duke of Wellington's Regiment (West Riding) (DWR): Halifax.

The Royal Hampshire Regiment.

The Staffordshire Regiment.

The Duke of Edinburgh's
Royal Regiment.

The Light Infantry.

The Royal Green Jackets.

The Prince of Wales' Division: Whittington Barracks, Lichfield, Staffs

1st Battalion The Devonshire & Dorset Regiment (D and D): Exeter.

1st Battalion The Cheshire Regiment (CHESHIRE): Chester.

1st Battalion The Royal Welch Fusiliers (RWF): Wrexham.

1st Battalion The Royal Regiment of Wales (24th/41st Foot) (RRW): Cardiff.

1st Battalion The Gloucestershire Regiment (GLOSTERS): Gloucester.

1st Battalion The Worcestershire & Sherwood Foresters Regiment (WFR) (29th/45th Foot): Worcester.

1st Battalion The Royal Hampshire Regiment (R HAMPS): Winchester.

1st Battalion The Staffordshire Regiment (The Prince of Wales') (STAFFORDS): Lichfield.

1st Battalion The Duke of Edinburgh's Royal Regiment (Berkshire and Wiltshire) (DERR): Salisbury.

The Light Division: Peninsula Barracks, Winchester, Hants

1st, 2nd and 3rd Battalions The Light Infantry (LI): Shrewsbury.

1st, 2nd and 3rd Battalions The Royal Green Jackets (RGJ): Winchester.